PARAGON
ISSUES IN
PHILOSOPHY

D1254175

PARAGON ISSUES IN PHILOSOPHY

PROBLEMS IN PERSONAL IDENTITY James Baillie

INDIVIDUAL, COMMUNITY, AND JUSTICE: ESSENTIAL READINGS IN SOCIAL AND POLITICAL PHILOSOPHY Jeffrey Barker and Evan McKenzie, Editors

PHILOSOPHY AND FEMINIST CRITICISM: AN INTRODUCTION Eve Browning Cole

PHILOSOPHY OF SCIENCE James Fetzer

FOUNDATIONS OF PHILOSOPHY OF SCIENCE: RECENT DEVELOPMENTS James Fetzer, Editor

PHILOSOPHY AND COGNITIVE SCIENCE James Fetzer

FOUNDATIONS OF COGNITIVE SCIENCE: THE ESSENTIAL READINGS Jay L. Garfield, Editor

MEANING AND TRUTH: ESSENTIAL READINGS IN MODERN SEMANTICS Jay L. Garfield and Murray Kiteley, Editors

LIVING THE GOOD LIFE: AN INTRODUCTION TO MORAL PHILOSOPHY Gordon Graham

PHILOSOPHY OF SPORT Drew Hyland

PHILOSOPHY OF TECHNOLOGY: AN INTRODUCTION Don Ihde

CRITICAL THEORY AND PHILOSOPHY David Ingram

CRITICAL THEORY: THE ESSENTIAL READINGS David Ingram and Julia Simon-Ingram, Editors

SOCIAL AND POLITICAL PHILOSOPHY William McBride

RACE, REASON, AND ORDER: PHILOSOPHY AND THE MODERN QUEST FOR SOCIAL ORDER Lucius Outlaw

METAPHYSICS: A CONTEMPORARY INTRODUCTION John Post

AFRICAN PHILOSOPHY: THE ESSENTIAL READINGS Tsenay Serequeberhan, Editor

INTRODUCTION TO MODERN SEMANTICS Ken Taylor

WOMAN AND THE HISTORY OF PHILOSOPHY Nancy Tuana

FORTHCOMING TITLES

HEART AND MIND: ESSAYS IN FEMINIST PHILOSOPHY Eve Browning Cole and Nancy Tuana, Editors

INTRODUCTION TO THE PHILOSOPHY OF LAW Vincent Wellman

THE PARAGON ISSUES IN PHILOSOPHY SERIES

At colleges and universities, interest in the traditional areas of philosophy remains strong. Many new currents flow within them, too, but some of these—the rise of cognitive science, for example, or feminist philosophy—went largely unnoticed in undergraduate philosophy courses until the end of the 1980s. The Paragon Issues in Philosophy Series responds to both perennial and newly influential concerns by bringing together a team of able philosophers to address the fundamental issues in philosophy today and to outline the state of contemporary discussion about them.

More than twenty volumes are scheduled; they are organized into three major categories. The first covers the standard topics—metaphysics, theory of knowledge, ethics, and political philosophy—stressing innovative developments in those disciplines. The second focuses on more specialized but still vital concerns in the philosophies of science, religion, history, sport, and other areas. The third category explores new work that relates philosophy and fields such as feminist criticism, medicine, economics, technology, and literature.

The level of writing is aimed at undergraduate students who have little previous experience studying philosophy. The books provide brief but accurate introductions that appraise the state of the art in their fields and show how the history of thought about their topics developed. Each volume is complete in itself but also complements others in the series.

Traumatic change characterizes these last years of the twentieth century: all of it involves philosophical issues. The editorial staff at

Paragon House has worked with us to develop this series. We hope it will encourage the understanding needed in our times, which are as complicated and problematic as they are promising.

John K. Roth   Frederick Sontag
Claremont McKenna College   Pomona College

PROBLEMS
IN
PERSONAL
IDENTITY

JAMES BAILLIE
UNIVERSITY OF
PORTLAND

PROBLEMS
IN
PERSONAL
IDENTITY

PARAGON
ISSUES IN
PHILOSOPHY

PARAGON HOUSE · NEW YORK

FIRST EDITION, 1993

PUBLISHED IN THE UNITED STATES BY

PARAGON HOUSE
90 FIFTH AVENUE
NEW YORK, N.Y. 10011

COPYRIGHT © 1993 BY PARAGON HOUSE

LIBRARY OF CONGRESS CATALOGING-IN-PUBLICATION DATA

BAILLIE, JAMES
    PROBLEMS IN PERSONAL IDENTITY/JAMES BAILLIE.
    P. CM.——(PARAGON ISSUES IN PHILOSOPHY)
    INCLUDES BIBLIOGRAPHICAL REFERENCES AND INDEX.
    ISBN 1-55778-521-X
    1. SELF (PHILOSOPHY) 2. SELF-KNOWLEDGE, THEORY OF. 3. IDENTITY
(PSYCHOLOGY) 4. CONSCIOUSNESS. I. TITLE. II. SERIES.
BD450. B257 1993
126—DC20

                                                    92-4995
                                                       CIP

MANUFACTURED IN THE UNITED STATES OF AMERICA

TO MY MOTHER

CONTENTS

ACKNOWLEDGMENTS   xiii

PREFACE   xv

CHAPTER 1 INTRODUCTION
Prelude • Varieties of Identity • Reductionism and Non-
Reductionism • Reductionist Criteria of Identity • The Menu   3

CHAPTER 2 IDENTITY AND SURVIVAL
Williams' Dilemma • The Closest Continuer Theory •
The Psychological Spectrum • The Physical Spectrum •
My Division • The 'Only X and Y' Rule • Appendix: Lewis—
The Indeterminacy of Population   12

CHAPTER 3 ASPECTS OF NON-REDUCTIONISM
Butler's Charge of Circularity • Quasi-Memory • Swinburne's
Simple View • Non-Reductionism and Dualism • The
Subjective View • Empirical Grounds for Non-Reductionism?   40

CHAPTER 4 WHAT AM I?
Introduction • Locke's Man/Person Distinction • Natural Kinds and
Natural Laws • Once an "f," Always an "f"? • Conditions of
Survival • Teletransportation Revisited • Is Identity Sortal-Relative?
• Appendix: Discontinuous Persons?   58

CHAPTER 5 METHODOLOGY MATTERS

Uses of Thought-Experiment • Abuses of Thought-Experiment • Human Freedom and Natural Laws • Thought-Experiments Reassessed • What Matters in Survival?   79

CHAPTER 6 MEMORY

Locke's Criterion • 'Memory' Dismantled • Memory Storage • Parfit's Psychological Criterion Tested • The Sleeping Pill • Varieties of Memory • Two Case Histories • Appendix: Psychogenic Fugue   98

CHAPTER 7 COMMISSUROTOMY AND THE UNITY OF MIND

Introduction • Commissurotomy Described • The Experimental Background • Minds, Brains, and Persons • Puccetti's 'Two Person' Theory • Cognition in the Right Hemisphere • Sperry's 'Two Mind' Theory • The Subjective View • Sperry Challenged • Split Brains and Single Minds • Appendix: My Physics Exam   114

CHAPTER 8 DEGREES OF PSYCHOLOGICAL INTEGRITY

MPD: Historical Background • Minds, Persons, and Personalities • Mary and Mary • All about Eve • Dissociation and Hypnosis • The Self • A Matter of Degree   141

IN CONCLUSION   158

SUGGESTED FURTHER READING   161

BIBLIOGRAPHY   163

INDEX OF NAMES   167

INDEX OF SUBJECTS   169

ACKNOWLEDGMENTS

■ wish to thank Mary Haight and Jim Edwards of the University of Glasgow, together with William Lyons of Trinity College, Dublin, for detailed comments on earlier versions of the material published here. My thanks are also due to the students in my "Problems of the Self" course at the University of Portland, particularly Susan Turvold. Explaining these ideas to them has clarified many issues for me. Finally, I am grateful to the editors of *The Philosophical Quarterly, Cogito, The Psychologist,* and *Journal of Philosophical Research* for permitting me to rework material that had previously been published in their journals.

James Baillie
Portland, Oregon
January 1992

PREFACE

This book is concerned with what it is to be a person, and with what is involved in being the same person over time. I begin by making a survey of the major theories of personal identity. I mark some important divisions and distinctions between them. Primarily, I distinguish Reductionism and Non-Reductionism and, within the former, between the Physical and the Psychological Criterion, and argue that none of these has proved to be satisfactory. I stress the importance of the work of Derek Parfit, and in particular his shifting of the agenda away from the relation of identity to that of 'Relation R,' and his claim that it is the holding of this latter relation—namely psychological continuity by any means—that contains 'all that matters' to us regarding the future, and not necessarily whether I survive. I show how this theory avoids the pitfalls that defeated the other theories, and propose various developments of it.

A critical eye is then cast over the methodology of thought-experimentation, so long the cornerstone of philosophical studies into personal identity, whereby conclusions are derived from considerations regarding what we would say if certain hypothetical states of affairs were to occur. The concept of 'theoretical possibility' is employed in order to determine the limits of applicability of such thought-experiments. Many influential arguments are found to be flawed due to misuse of this methodology.

The remainder of the book is concerned with identifying and discussing issues that remain once a more modest methodological framework is imposed. These concern the nature and the limits of psychological unity and continuity. They focus on real-life conditions, both typical and pathological, and are rooted within scientific research rather than in imaginative speculation.

My conclusions are for the most part negative, arguing that not only the answers but also the questions that have traditionally been posed regarding personal identity cease to be relevant, once the flaws in the framework that supported them have been exposed.

PROBLEMS
IN
PERSONAL
IDENTITY

CHAPTER ONE

INTRODUCTION

PRELUDE

■ was initially drawn into investigations of personal identity
through my fascination with the work of Derek Parfit, and his
iconoclastic claim that identity itself was not essentially 'what matters' regarding the future. In my initial studies, I saw my task as in
developing a Parfitian theory. In doing so, I wholeheartedly adopted
the method of thought-experimentation, as employed by my mentor
and so many of his illustrious peers and predecessors. However, in
time I began to have serious misgivings over this methodology. It
seemed to me that some of the most famous thought-experiments
were firstly too outlandish and secondly too vague (and that these
two factors were integrally connected) to admit trustworthy conclusions.

Wittgenstein famously described the situation of someone
bewitched by a misleading philosophical perspective as being akin
to a fly trapped in a bottle, forever buzzing around in circles in the
illusion of progress, but who only needed to stop and look up for
the way out to come into view and be seen to have been there all
along. While identifying with this picture, a more accurate
metaphor for my own predicament is that of a fly who has been
enticed by a drop of jam, and who, finding himself stuck to it, is left
with the only option of eating himself free. This is the project of the
first half of this book—that of working from within the tradition of
thought-experimentation, devouring its choice delicacies, even
making a few of my own, and concluding that while the feast is

very tasty and enjoyable, it is excessive and in need of the application of a few principles of sound nutrition.

However, rather than urging an outright rejection of the practice, I advocate extreme caution in its employment. Whilst some notable examples are rejected, I keep an open mind regarding others, and admit that the situations described therein might conceivably be actualized. In the second half of the book, I identify and investigate the issues that remain once the unrestricted use of thought-experiment is rejected. As we will see, I argue that many of the traditional issues dominating the subject should be dropped, as they gained credence from a discredited approach. Thus the whole basis of inquiry into personal identity needs to be reassessed.

In this introductory chapter I will give a brief overview of the dominant theories and analyses of personal identity, and describe some important distinctions and classifications employed in the construction of these theories. This will enable me to set the scene for the more detailed investigations of the following chapters.

VARIETIES OF IDENTITY

In any discussion of personal identity, and of identity in general, there are several different concepts that must be clearly distinguished, since confusing them can lead to profound error. It is best to make these distinctions clearly at the beginning. Firstly, when psychologists (and indeed the general public) speak of one's identity, they are dealing with the way one conceives of oneself. For instance, I might view myself in terms of categories such as Scottish, male, white, liberal, intellectual, and suchlike. Philosophers are *not* primarily concerned with 'identity' in this sense. Rather, the philosophical concept of identity derives from logic. Logicians regard identity as an *equivalence relation*, that is, it comprises the following relations:

> *reflexivity:* $x = x$
> *symmetry:* if $x = y$, then $y = x$
> *transitivity:* if $x = y$, and $y = z$, then $x = z$.

However, the crucial property that distinguishes identity statements from all others is that they obey *Leibniz' Law,* otherwise known as the law of the *Indiscernibility of Identicals,* i.e., if $x = y$, then whatever is true of x is true of y and vice versa. For example, assuming that Bob Dylan and Robert Zimmerman are the same person, if Dylan can't sing, then neither can Zimmerman.

The type of identity referred to in the above specifications is *numerical identity,* and must be distinguished from *qualitative identity,* otherwise known as 'exact similarity.' (When the term 'identity' appears on its own, I take it to refer to numerical identity.) If x and y are numerically identical, then they are one and the same thing. However, if x and y are qualitatively identical, then they are exactly alike in their intrinsic properties and qualities, but it does not follow that they are numerically identical. Rather, this relationship can be expressed by saying that x and y are tokens of the same type. For example, two cans of tomato soup can be qualitatively identical. Likewise, so would two prints of a Warhol painting of these cans.

Many philosophical quandaries arise from confusing or running together these concepts of numerical and qualitative identity. The difficulties are compounded by yet another distinction, that of *synchronic* and *diachronic* identity. If x and y are synchronically identical, then they are numerically identical (i.e., one and the same thing) at any given time t; whereas if x and y are diachronically identical, then the relation of numerical identity holds between them over time. That is, they are stages or 'time-slices' of the same temporally-enduring object. For example, you-as-a-baby and you-right-now are stages of the same person.

In cases concerning the alleged holding of synchronic identity, the content of the question 'is $a = b$?' often unpacks to reveal a question regarding sense and reference, i.e., whether 'a' and 'b' are terms that refer to the same object but under different descriptions, or having distinct causal chains of usage, grounded in the same object. For example, let 'a' and 'b' stand for 'Bob Dylan' and 'Robert Zimmerman' respectively. If someone asks, "Is Robert Zimmerman really Bob Dylan," the person is unlikely to be posing some deep metaphysical enquiry, but merely asking whether these two names refer to the same guy. In recent years, another set of problems relating to the synchronic identity of persons has come to the fore, concerning such phenomena as split-brain surgery and Multiple Personality Disorder. These conditions raise difficult questions about the concept of the 'unity of mind,' and about the copersonality relation among mental states. In other words, the question is, Under what conditions are mental states attributable to the same person at any given time? I discuss these issues in detail in the final two chapters.

However, it is undoubtedly the case that the majority of the perennial questions regarding identity, and particularly personal identity, have been posed in regard to matters concerning diachronic identity. The basic fact that everything in the Universe is in motion and constantly undergoing changes raises the fundamental question of how and under what conditions can identity be maintained through time in the absence or breaching of qualitative identity, in the face of such unremitting change. Clearly no one would suggest that identity is preserved throughout all possible changes, so we must closely examine the issues regarding the criteria for identity through time for specific classes of entities.

It is wise to clear up some potential confusion regarding the relationship of Leibniz' Law to diachronic identity. To take an example: the newspaper, a copy of which was purchased by my father, that announced my birth to a jubilant world was, on that day *(t1)*, clean and white. That paper is now *(t2)* dirty, yellow, and crumpled, in a cupboard in my mother's house. Let us call the hot-off-the-press paper *'a'* and the old rag *'b'*. I want to say that $a = b$. But does not Leibniz' Law demand that if $a = b$, then any property that can be ascribed to a must equally be ascribable to *b?* And surely a is white and b is not?

Such an argument misapplies Leibniz' Law. I accept that if the paper is white at *t1* and not white at *t2*, then there is a true predication of it at *t1* that is a false predication of it at *t2*. However, this does not contravene Leibniz' Law, as this law does not require that if $a = b$, then if a is W (white) at *t1* then b is W at *t2*, but that if a is W at *t1*, then b is W at t1.

REDUCTIONISM AND NON-REDUCTIONISM

Throughout this book I shall be referring to theories of personal identity as being either a Reductionist or a Non-Reductionist criterion. This is probably the most fundamental way of classifying criteria of personal identity, and it is critically important to have a grasp of the distinction at the outset, so I shall state it fairly explicitly and expansively.

A *Reductionist* theory of personal identity comprises the following claims:

1. The fact of the holding of personal identity through time consists purely in the holding of *other* facts, concerning physical and/or psychological continuity.

2. A person's existence consists merely in the existence of a brain and body, and the occurrence of a causally interrelated set of mental and physical states.

3. While persons can be said to exist, and to *have* experiences, they are not 'separately existing entities' over and above those existents specified in 2.

4. These facts in which personal identity consists can be described 'impersonally,' that is, without attributing them to any person. Thus, while persons exist in the sense described in 3, we could give a complete description of reality without mentioning persons.

5. There can be cases in which it is 'unpuzzlingly indeterminate' whether or not $x(t1)$ is the same person as $y(t2)$. Still, numerical identity is an 'all or nothing' relation that does not admit of degrees. Rather, the point relates to 3—since persons are not separately existing entities, the relation of personal identity can be reduced and redescribed in terms of physical and/or psychological continuity; and since these relations do admit of degrees, there may be cases where we cannot supply a clear answer regarding identity. However, this indeterminacy is a *semantic* matter, not a metaphysical one. There is no indeterminacy built into reality concerning whether or not some a at $t1$ is the same person as some b at $t2$. Rather, in such cases there is an indeterminacy in the conditions of application of the descriptive term (often called the 'sortal concept') covering a and b. 'Person' is a *vague* concept—i.e., there is

no clear rule specifying all conditions under which one does or does not count as a person, or as the same person over time. While most real-life cases will be unproblematic, there is always the possibility of a problematic, indeterminate 'grey area.'

6. In such situations, and when all the facts of the matter are known, then any remaining question concerning identity is an *empty* question. That is, it is not a genuine question regarding different possibilities, but a case where apparently conflicting answers are only different descriptions of the same facts.

7. Parfit has made the further claim that what fundamentally matters regarding the future is not whether or not *I* survive. In other words, the relation that contains all that matters is not identity, but *Relation R,* i.e., psychological continuity by any means (I discuss all this shortly). So when we know whether someone survives at a later date who is psychologically continuous with me now, we know enough to determine all that matters regarding the future, even if the question of identity remains.

While the majority of contemporary theorists are Reductionists of some sort, there is room for significant disagreements among them. My description of Reductionism most closely resembles the view of Derek Parfit. I would say that all Reductionists accept 1–3, so that these combined theses probably constitute the core of the Reductionist position. At least one theorist, Thomas Nagel [1986], would resist 4. Theses 5 and 6 would be resisted by David Wiggins [1980], who holds that the survival of a full human consciousness and more than half a brain constitute necessary and sufficient conditions for identity over time. Finally, as we shall see, 7 is the most controversial claim of them all.

A *Non-Reductionist* theory of personal identity can be defined in terms of its opposition to this Reductionist creed. In particular, Non-Reductionism holds that:

1. Persons are separately existing basic entities apart from a body and brain and sets of mental and physical states.

2. Personal identity is a 'further fact,' irreducible to these other facts.

3. The holding (or not) of identity through time is necessarily a determinate matter.

4. My survival is essentially what matters to me regarding the future.

Parfit remarks that once these conditions are combined, Non-Reductionism appears to be ontologically committed to something like a Cartesian Ego. However, in saying that questions of identity must admit of a determinate answer, Non-Reductionism isn't committed to saying that we can always in fact know this answer. It is only committed to a realism about such facts, in the sense that such 'further facts' exist, even if they transcend our practical limitations on verification. So, for example, a Kantian belief in a Transcendental Ego located within an unknowable Noumenal world would still count as a Non-Reductionist theory.

REDUCTIONIST CRITERIA OF IDENTITY

Reductionism is by far the dominant perspective, and most interesting debates take place within its confines. The basic dispute is between the *Physical and Psychological Criteria.* Both theories have a long philosophical pedigree, but in their modern variants are not committed to much of the metaphysical baggage carried by their older formulations. For instance, the issue of dualism versus materialism has been set aside, as contemporary Reductionists are all committed to some form of materialism. Rather, the two criteria differ by focussing on different levels of description of the events constitutive of identity, or they disagree over the priority of certain events in weighing considerations of identity.

I will not dwell over the relative merits of numerous subtly different formulations of each criterion. Rather, I will confine myself to stating both criteria in what I regard as the most plausible forms, and indicate their strengths.

The Physical Criterion can be stated as follows:

x (t1) is the same person as y (t2) if and only if enough of x's brain survives at t2, and has the capacity to support a full human consciousness, and is now y's brain; and if no other person z (t2) exists who also has enough of x's brain to support a full human consciousness.

For the moment, note that this is a rather sophisticated version of the criterion, with its emphasis on the brain, rather than the body per se. Note also that it is committed to the spatio-temporal continuity of the brain as a necessary condition of identity through time. I will attempt to refute this latter thesis in Chapter 4.

The Psychological Criterion can be stated thus:

x (t1) is the same person as y (t2) if and only if x is psychologically continuous with y, and with no other z (t2).

The most influential formulation of this criterion has come from Parfit, and I will employ some of his vocabulary to discuss it. The brevity of this criterion is misleading in its apparent simplicity, and its sophistication is revealed when we unpack the key notion of psychological continuity. Firstly, *psychological connectedness* consists in the holding of particular direct psychological connections between mental events. The paradigm cases offered by Parfit are between an experience and the subsequent memory of it, or between the forming of an intention and the subsequent acting on it. Connectedness is a relation that comes by degrees, depending on the number of direct connections that hold. *Strong connectedness* holds in cases where at least half the number of direct connections are preserved until at least the next day.

We can now define *psychological continuity* as consisting in overlapping chains of strong connectedness. This preserves personal identity through time in cases where there is an absence of a suitable degree of psychological connectedness holding over longer periods of time than a day. Thus it avoids the paradox threatened by Reid's example (see Chapter 6) of the officer who remembers stealing apples as a child but who, as a general in later life, remembers having led a cavalry charge as an officer, but not having stolen the apples. So, although most experiences occurring around *t1* will be forgotten at *t100,* they will be mostly remembered at *t2* (i.e., the following day), and most experiences at *t2* will be remembered at *t3,* and so on. So we have overlapping chains of memories that preserve our psychological continuity, and, thereby, our identity.

Different versions of the Psychological Criterion disagree over the issue of which causal processes can be responsible for the maintenance of psychological continuity. The *Narrow* Psychological Criterion admits only the normal cause—one continuously functioning brain—as suitable. By contrast, the *Wide* Psychological Criterion allows *any* causal process that permits psychological continuity to hold. So, for example, in the teletransportation examples so loved by philosophers (see Chapter 4), the Wide Psychological Criterion would permit my replica and I to be identified, but neither the Physical Criterion nor the Narrow Psychological Criterion would agree.

THE MENU

Chapter 2.   I continue to investigate the dispute between the Physical and Psychological Criteria by offering a critical discussion of some of the major contemporary contributions to the debate.

Chapter 3.   I discuss aspects of Non-Reductionism.

Chapter 4.   I pick up the thread of Chapter 2, with particular reference to the issue of sortal-covered identity statements, and the question, "What kind of thing am I?"

Chapter 5.   I question the methodology of thought-experimentation that has figured heavily in the preceding chapters.

Chapter 6.   I investigate psychological continuity with reference to the central concept of memory.

Chapter 7.   I discuss the implications of split-brain surgery for the concept of mental unity.

Chapter 8.   I continue this discussion by investigating issues deriving Multiple Personality Disorder.

Conclusions.

CHAPTER TWO

IDENTITY AND SURVIVAL

As an entry into the contemporary debate between the Physical and Psychological Criteria, I will describe a puzzle set by Williams [1970], which goes directly to the heart of the matter. I will follow this with an influential response from Nozick [1981], followed by another more fruitful reply by Parfit.

WILLIAMS' DILEMMA

In previous publications, Bernard Williams had advocated a form of the Physical Criterion, but by the time he had published "The Self and the Future" [1970], his perception of the issues had grown considerably more sophisticated, as this article provides an argument that seems to cast doubt on both the Physical and Psychological Criteria. Williams describes a thought-experiment in which it seems that one person has 'swapped' his original body and brain for another, and survives as the same person in this new body. Such an example clearly points in favor of the Psychological Criterion. However, he then devises another thought-experiment that points firmly to the Physical Criterion. The trouble is that this latter case is very similar to the previous one, to the extent of being merely an alternative description of the same state of affairs. How then can it lead to a contrary conclusion?

The examples involve that old and trusted friend of philosophers, the mad neuroscientist. In Case 1, this highly disagreeable fellow has captured two persons, *A* and *B,* and performs what might be described as a 'mind-swap' on them. In other words, he employs some technology to 'record' their entire respective sets of memories, character traits, etc. He erases these mental states from their respective brains, and then 'switches' them, so that the mental states that had been realized by *A's* brain are now realized within *B's* brain, and vice versa. The resulting persons are called the '*A*-body-person' and the '*B*-body-person'—i.e., the *A*-body-person is the person whose present body was once *A*'s body, and the *B*-body-person is likewise related to *B*.

Clearly, the big question concerns diachronic identity—are *A* and the *A*-body person stages of the same temporally-enduring person, or are *A* and the *B*-body person? (As shorthand, I will use the more manageable expressions 'is identical with,' or '=' in tackling this issue. So the question is whether *A* = the *A*-body-person or the *B*-body-person.) Prior to the operation, *A* and *B* are told that one of the resulting persons will be given $100,000, whilst the other will be tortured. They are asked to choose who will get what, by basing their decision purely on self-interest. If *A* and *B* both thought that the operation constituted a mind-swap (or, equally, a 'body-swap'), then *A* would choose that the *B*-body-person get the money and that the *A*-body-person be tortured. *B* would choose the opposite. Williams plausibly argues that if the scientist withholds his decision from them until he actually carries it out by torturing the *B*-body-person and paying the *A*-body-person, then the *B*-body-person, having *A's* memories, will complain that that wasn't the outcome that he had chosen. Meanwhile, the *A*-body-person will be relieved that his choice, as *B,* was selected.

In fact, the claim that *A* = the *B*-body-person and that *B* = the *A*-body-person looks justified even if both victims don't view the operation as a mind-swap. For example, if *A* supports a Physical Criterion, he will choose that the *B*-body person is tortured. Still, as Williams suggests, he, *as* the *B*-body person, will soon realize his error once the torture begins. More precisely, he will recognize the unfortunate choice as being *his*.

In Case 2, *I* have been captured by this same mad scientist, who plans to use me as the subject of his dastardly experiments. I am informed that I am to be subjected to agonizing torture, prior to which all my mental states—my memories, character traits, likes and dislikes, etc.—will be erased from my mind, so that I will forget that I am about to be tortured. In addition, my lost 'mental set' will be replaced with another set of memories, etc., that are qualitatively identical to those of some *other* person. As Williams argues, when I anticipate all these forthcoming experiences, it is plausible to assume that the knowledge that I will undergo all these psychological changes would not remove nor lessen my fear of the imminent torture, nor my conviction that it is still *I* who is to suffer, despite all these changes. In fact, these changes seem to *add* to my ordeal, as I not only have to cope with physical agony, but also mental derangement.

Given that Case 2 involves a complete break in psychological continuity, the Psychological Criterion would recommend that I not be egotistically concerned with the person who will occupy my body after the psychological changes, since he and I are not the same person. However, as Williams says, our intuitions are clear that it is I who is to be tortured. Thus our fear appears well-justified and the Psychological Criterion, it now seems, does not. Yet surely Case 2 is only a redescription of Case 1, stated in first person singular terms. Thus, if I call myself '*A*,' then the conclusion is that *A* = the *A*-body-person, in contrast to the previous conclusion.

The other difference between the two cases is that in Case 2 the second person involved, the 'mind-donor,' is depicted as playing a minor part, and the implication is that anything happening to *him* cannot affect the purported *A:A*-body-person identification. This argument is supported by two principles suggested by Williams in a previous essay [1957]. The first principle states that whether x *(t1)* is identical with y *(t2)* can only depend on facts concerning x and y. Facts concerning some other z are irrelevant. The second principle is that if x *(t1)* is identical with y *(t2)* by virtue of some relation holding between them, there cannot be any other z who is similarly related to x at $t2$. If z does exist, or even could have existed, then x and y are not to be identified.

In Case 1, what happens to the second person is crucial because

we seemed forced to conclude that I am identical to the person surviving in his body after the operation. Yet from the perspective of
Case 2, even if we bring the two cases more into line by allowing
my original 'mental set' to be realized in some other body, it still
makes no difference to what will happen to me. I am to be tortured,
no matter what happens to anyone else. So Williams has presented
us with an antinomy, as we have been led to two mutually exclusive
conclusions on the basis of the same premises. Williams admits
himself to be puzzled, and offers no solution.

THE CLOSEST CONTINUER THEORY

Robert Nozick suggests a way of compatibilizing our divergent
responses to the two cases, by denying Williams' above-mentioned
principles. Nozick claims that the issue of whether x $(t1)$ and y $(t2)$
are identical will always depend on who or what else is present at
$t2$. Nozick offers the Closest Continuer theory. It can be described
thus: x $(t1)$ is identical with y $(t2)$ if y's properties are causally
dependent on x's, and if no other z $(t2)$ stands in a closer (or as
close) relation to x. Corollary to this 'closest continuer' relation is
the 'closest predecessor' relation, whereby $x = y$ if x is y's closest
predecessor. In other words, y cannot more closely continue some
other z $(t1)$ than it does x. If x is y's closest predecessor and y is x's
closest continuer, then x and y are said to be 'mono-related,' i.e.,
identical.

   Nozick thinks that we actually do (presumably unconsciously)
make judgments concerning identity in accordance with his theory.
He also claims that its responses to philosophical 'problem cases'
(e.g., Williams) accord with our intuitions. However, he then back-
tracks significantly to say that the theory alone cannot solve all
problems of identity, as it does not specify *"what dimension or
weighed sum of dimensions measures closeness"* (p. 33). Take the
famous example of the ship of Theseus. In the course of time, a
ship gradually has all its parts replaced, so that eventually not one
original part remains. Yet throughout this time it has remained
afloat and functioning as a ship, and still bears the same name.

However, in the intervening period, the original parts were being collected. Once the entire set has been gathered, a shipbuilder restores them to their former functions, and launches the reassembled ship. So now we have two ships, each with a claim to be identical through time with the original one. In Nozick's terms, the 'dimensions' against which identity-claims are to be assessed are firstly spatio-temporal continuity as a functioning ship, and secondly numerical identity of parts. But, as Nozick himself has admitted, he cannot tell us which of these should take priority.

This example may seem to be extremely contrived and fantastic, but structurally similar examples do occasionally occur. Take the recent case of the rock band 'Yes.' The band was originally formed in the late 1960s, but their greatest commercial and artistic successes were in the early 1970s, so that this version of the band is widely considered to be the definitive lineup. These musicians gradually left and were replaced, so that by the late 1980s only one original member remained. By this time, the other four members of the definitive lineup had regrouped, and planned to present themselves under the name 'Yes,' only to be blocked by the remaining member who claimed that this name was rightfully his. So, as in the case of the ships, we now have two bands both claiming to be the 'real Yes.' One band's case rests on their continuity of function as a band throughout the various replacements, whereas the other band's claim is based on the numerical identity through time of (most of) the definitive members. Again, the Closest Continuer theory can give no guidance as to which of these two 'dimensions of closeness' should take priority. Still, this case had a happy ending with a financially rewarding compromise when they chose to embark on a highly profitable tour featuring all members, past and present. This solution was sadly unavailable for the would-be ships of Theseus.

Also, the Closest Continuer theory can at most offer a necessary, but not a sufficient condition of identity, as y can be x's closest continuer, yet not be close enough to x for the identity relation to hold. This 'minimum closeness requirement,' and the dimensions along which it is measured, will vary according to the kind of object under question, says Nozick.

Nozick lists a number of classic puzzles to demonstrate that his solutions to them accord with our intuitive responses. For example, if *A (t1)* has his brain-states taped and programmed into a clone body, then this clone, *B,* is not identical to *A,* as *A's* closest continuer at *t2* is *A* himself. However, if *A* were to die during the brain-state transfer, then *B would* be *A's* closest continuer due to the psychological continuity between them. Thus *B* would be identical with *A.*

Nozick never spells out his solution to Williams' dilemma. However, it seems to be that in Case 2, *A's* concern for the *A*-body-person is due to the fact that this person is, in the absence of anyone else, *A's* closest continuer. On the other hand, In Case 1, psychological continuity overrules this physical continuity so that the *B*-body-person is *A's* closest continuer. This, of course, gets us nowhere. It merely restates the problem, namely, given that the two cases are virtually alternative descriptions of the same type of situation, how do they lead us to such opposite conclusions? Why do two different 'dimensions' take precedence in these cases? I will have more to say on Williams' poser later in this chapter, and also in Chapter 5, where I argue that its real significance is very different from that which Williams intends. But firstly I will continue my criticisms of the Closest Continuer theory.

Not only do I deny that it is always in accordance with our intuitions, but I also argue that it gets itself into such a muddle in trying to do so that it loses all credibility. One type of situation that exposes the theory's weakness is that of a 'tie.' This is a case where *both* *y* and *z* at *t2* are equally close continuers of *x (t1),* along the same dimensions. Nozick stresses that his theory is strictly a *Closest* Continuer theory, which does not admit identity with a mere 'continuer none is closer than.' Thus he claims that *neither y* nor *z* is *x's* closest continuer, and thus that *x* ceases to exist.

So for example in Parfit's [1984] story 'My Division' (p. 254), in which *A's* cerebral hemispheres are removed, separated, and transplanted into the vacant skulls of his triplet siblings *B* and *C, A* ceases to exist. This is surely counterintuitive, given the physical continuity and the subsequent psychological continuity provided by each hemisphere. Nozick is driven to his conclusion by the fact that all alternatives seem to him to be even more hopeless. For example, *B and C* cannot *both* be identical with *A*, as it would then follow from the transitivity of the identity relation that *B* and *C* would be identical with each other, and they obviously are not. Neither can it be that *one* of *B* and *C* is identical with *A*. Since *B* and *C* are qualitatively identical, and are causally related to *A* in exactly the same way, any reason for identifying *A* with one of them must equally be a reason for identifying *A* with the other one. And clearly one is not justified in just stipulating that *A* is identical with one of them, but for no reason.

However, surely Nozick's own solution is equally hopeless. If *A* is not identical with either *B* or *C*, then he shouldn't be self-interestedly concerned with whatever happens to either of them. So if he is told that *B* will be tortured in the near future, he shouldn't be concerned for *B* in any way over and above the humanitarian concern for another person, or even the added concern for friends or relations. But we are strongly inclined to say that *A* would, and should, be self-interestedly concerned for *B*.

Nozick tries to deal with this difficulty by saying that the degree of care that any *x (t1)* feels for any *y (t2)* will be proportional to the closeness between them among the appropriate dimensions, with the exception of cases where *y* is *x*'s closest continuer, as *x* cares about his closest continuer in a special way, not proportional to closeness (as long as *y* satisfies the minimum closeness requirement). So he seems to be saying that *A* will not be concerned with ceasing to exist, as what matters in this situation is that someone exists who continues *A* closely enough to have been identical to *A* if he had been his closest continuer. So, in such a tie situation, *A* will be equally concerned about *B* and *C*, and in proportion to their closeness to him. However, had *B* been his closest continuer, yet intrinsically no closer to *A* than in the tie situation, then the degree of concern accorded to him would increase.

Nozick next considers cases involving 'overlap.' Suppose that one of my cerebral hemispheres is transplanted into a clone body, and I retain the other one. Next, suppose that I die at a later date, so that there is a partial overlap in our lifetimes. Now if I had died immediately following the hemispherectomy, we would say that the clone is my closest continuer, and thus identical with me. Yet, according to Nozick, if I had survived for several more years, then I (i.e., in my original body) would be my closest continuer within that time, and secondly, the clone would not become identical with me after my death. But clearly the idea of a sharp dividing line specifying the amount of overlap that cannot be crossed if the clone and I are to be identified is absurd.

Surely this example exposes Nozick's theory to the same problems as those he rejects. He tries to evade the trap by saying that the problem is due to a tension between the Closest Continuer theory in firstly its 'local' form (i.e., the theory described in previous paragraphs), and secondly its 'global' form. The global variant states that x $(t1)$ is identical y $(t2)$ if y is x's closest continuer and if there is no more extended thing z which is more closely continuous with x than any other equally extended thing of which x is a part. So in an overlap situation as illustrated below (where A represents myself before the hemispherectomy, B is myself after the operation, C is the clone while I am alive, and D is the clone after I am dead),

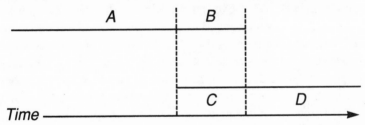

we have a situation where

        i. B is A's closest continuer, and
        ii. D is the closest continuer of $A+B$, yet
        iii. C is D's closest predecessor, and
        iv. A is the closest predecessor of $C+D$.

So neither $A+B+D$ nor $A+C+D$ are mono-related, and cannot be stages of the same continuous person. However, A and D are mono-related, and the global theory says that where B and C are relatively small compared to the timespan of A and D, then $A+D$ constitute a single person, albeit a temporally discontinuous one.

The first thing to say about this attempted solution is that Nozick can no longer claim to have the support of our intuitions. Our intuitions are simple fellows, and Nozick's theory grows more convoluted by the minute. More seriously, his ad hoc introduction of the global variant does nothing to deal with the absurdities of the 'sharp dividing line' that scuppered the local theory. All it does, at best, is to provide an illustration of the Closest Continuer theory's inadequacies.

THE PSYCHOLOGICAL SPECTRUM

My own view is that if you regard these hypothetical 'problem cases' as having any real bearing on issues of identity, then any attempt to deal with these cases in terms of the concept of identity will fail, and that a more fruitful approach is to follow Parfit's line and analyze them in terms of 'Relation R' or, as Brennan [1988] does, 'survival.' The Closest Continuer theory can retain its insights when it is interpreted as a theory of the conditions of *survival* rather than of identity. Briefly, x's closest continuer is whoever survives x to the greatest degree; in cases of a tie, there is a 'double success' rather than both candidates cancelling each other out, as when the cases are described in terms of identity. I discuss Brennan and his concept of survival in Chapter 4, but for the moment I will concentrate on Parfit.

Let us now consider Parfit's response to Williams' Case 2, which pointed to a Physical Criterion. Parfit develops Williams' story to devise a whole range of cases (called 'the Psychological Spectrum'), each involving some degree of disruption of psychological continuity. Williams' own case is at the far end of the spectrum, as it involves a total break of psychological continuity. A near-end case would involve minimal loss of memories, character traits, etc., and correspondingly minimal addition of new ones. Between these extremes would be a vast number of cases, each involving a tiny amount more psychological change than its predecessor.

Parfit employs the ancient Greek 'Sorites' argument, or 'the paradox of the heap': Imagine a heap of sand, comprising 100,000 grains. Now take one grain away. It seems obvious that the remaining 99,999 grains still constitute a heap—after all, how could such an infinitesimal loss make any real difference? The same reasoning applies if one further grain is removed, and so on. However, by repeated applications of this operation, we arrive at the absurd conclusion that *one* grain of sand constitutes a heap, since there appears to be no point at which one particular grain (e.g., the 65th, or the 10th) is decisive to heaphood. So we start with a true premise, apply an apparently reasonable principle (i.e., that the removal of one grain cannot make a decisive difference to whether or not it remains a heap), yet arrive at a falsehood. The problem occurs, of course, because 'heap' is a vague concept. I must stress that the point is not that no one knows the moment at which the sand ceases to be a heap, but that there is no fact of the matter here.

As with the case of the Ship of Theseus, this example is not as contrived and unusual as it first appears. In fact, most predicates (outside the strictly defined terms of the natural sciences) have some degree of vagueness. Here is an example that will make these issues clearer. To my deep regret, I began to lose my hair at a young age. The rate of hair loss has been slow but relentless, and I expect to be undeniably bald in another ten years. So let us accept that it will be true at that time to say that I am bald at the age of 45. Now contrast my proudly hirsute self at 20. Clearly I am not bald at this time. Let us suppose that each day I lose, on average, fifty more hairs than are replaced. Nevertheless, by the next day I am obviously not bald. The loss of fifty hairs is not sufficient to turn a hairy young man into a prematurely bald one. Likewise, on the next day, and the day after that, etc., etc., my baldness will remain a future terror rather than a present curse.

The paradox should now be obvious: if this hair loss continues long enough, then my head will eventually be completely devoid of hair—yet we never reach any point during this time at which we can plausibly say, "Well, he's not bald yet, but he will be if fifty more hairs go!" Likewise, given this uniformity in the rate of hair loss, I will not wake some morning with a newly acquired baldness. There is far too little qualitative difference in my appearance over any two contiguous days to ever justify saying "Hair today, gone tomorrow." So the concept of baldness has no precise conditions of applicability, and is thus a vague concept. This is no consolation to me.

Parfit applies this line of reasoning to the Psychological Spectrum. Let us begin with the extreme near-end case, involving minimal change, and let us call the pre-operative person 'A' and the post-operative person 'B.' If we agree, as seems extremely plausible, that A and B are the same person, then, given that the spectrum can contain any number of possible cases according to how close we make contiguous cases, then if the next case (calling the first one 'n' and the next one '$n+1$') involves an infinitesimal increase in psychological change to what occurred in case n, then surely $A = B$ in case $n+1$, as there is virtually no difference between the cases. Someone taking this line could draw on Williams' [1957] rule that something so important as a loss of identity could not rest on such as insignificant matter as the negligible difference between cases n and $n+1$. However, the paradox arises when we apply this procedure to each consecutive pair of cases right through the spectrum. This seems to force us into concluding that $A = B$ even in the extreme far-end of the spectrum case, where there is *no* psychological continuity between A and B.

At this point it looks as if Parfit is just agreeing With Williams regarding the weakness of the Psychological Criterion. This appearance is deceptive, as Parfit's argument so far is merely a prelude to his main thesis and its far more radical conclusion. Before leaving the Psychological Spectrum for the moment, it is instructive to note that Parfit could have pushed his argument harder to allow the paradoxes to pile up. Let us apply the Sorites argument again, but starting this time with Williams' extreme far-end Case 2 (let us call it $n+100$). If a defender of the Psychological Criterion says that $A \neq B$ in such a case, then he seems obliged to make the same judgment in the second-last case, $n+9$, and likewise all the way back down the spectrum to case n. So here we have obtained the opposite conclusion to Parfit (i.e., $A \neq B$ in case n) by another application of the same technique.

THE PHYSICAL SPECTRUM

Parfit comments that the paradox he has exposed is not primarily due to any flaw unique to the Psychological Criterion, but is due to the underlying assumption that there must be a determinate answer to questions of identity through time in all possible cases. He attacks this assumption, arguing that in at least some central cases in the Psychological Spectrum, any such questions are empty. He then turns the tables on the Physical Criterion by showing that it is equally vulnerable to paradox, by applying a similar form of argument as before, if we accept the assumption that identity is always a determinate issue.

A 'Physical Spectrum' is devised, wherein a scale of minute gradations of change are applied to $A's$ body, his brain and body cells being replaced by exact duplicates. So in the extreme near-end case n we have a person B who is virtually both physically and psychologically continuous with A (on the assumption that psychological properties are supervenient on physical properties), and thus we seem to have overwhelming reason to say that $A = B$. In the far-end case, B will be completely psychologically continuous with A, but will not be in any way physically continuous, as 100% of his cells have been simultaneously destroyed and replaced. Thus in this case, a necessary condition of the Physical Criterion is broken, so it forces us to say that $A \neq B$. As Unger [1990] remarks, physical continuity might be maintained if the cell-replacement had occurred very gradually, thus allowing each new input of cells to become integrated with the preexisting structures.

A supporter of the Physical Criterion who also held that identity was always a determinate matter would then be committed to the claim that identity is preserved only if a critical percentage of cells remains unreplaced. But how can we establish this critical percentage of cells in a way that is not arbitrary and stipulative? No independent test could ever confirm or falsify the credentials of such a choice. The only possible independent test would have to come from *B's* own testimony. But since *A* and *B* are completely psychologically continuous in all cases of the spectrum, *B* will always claim to be the same person as *A*. Thus Parfit's argument pushes us towards accepting a *wide* Psychological Criterion.

Parfit goes on to consider a variant on the Physical Criterion deriving from the then unpublished work by Thomas Nagel. (Nagel's most recent views were subsequently published in 1986.) Nagel is a Reductionist who thinks that I am essentially my brain. He also holds that identity is the relation that contains 'all that matters' in my self-interested concern for the future. Parfit tries to expose the inconsistency of this position by means of another thought-experiment: I have been diagnosed as having a potentially fatal brain disease that requires immediate treatment. I have the choice of two operations, wherein my neurons are replaced by non-diseased neurons that will allow full psychological continuity to be maintained. The first operation, *01,* is really a sequence of one hundred mini-operations each involving the removal of 1% of my brain, and replacement by appropriate neurons. The second operation, *02,* involves the removal of the entire brain in a single move, and the transplant of a whole new brain.

In *01,* each new percentage of replacement neurons becomes structurally and functionally integrated with the original brain, and thus can be legitimately regarded as *part* of this brain, and thus of preserving my identity throughout the part-replacement. (Incidentally, one can easily construct an analogue to the puzzle of the ship of Theseus by supposing that some scientist kept the original cells, keeping them alive and reassembling them in a clone body.) However, the situation is different in *02,* as the original brain has been destroyed. Parfit claims that Nagel must say that I survive in *01* but not in *02.* But since there is full psychological continuity in both cases, surely the difference in how this is achieved is a trivial matter that cannot mean the difference between life and death.

Brennan, while defending a generally Parfitian theory, argues that we needn't see *02* as involving the destruction of my brain, since according to his 'conditions of survival' (see Chapter 4), my brain survives to a high degree in its replica. The production of this replica is a *copying process* using my original brain as the prototype. Thus the two brains are causally related. We can make the additional point that my brain and its replica in *02* are two tokens of the type 'my brain.'

John Robinson offers a telling counterexample to Parfit's Physical Spectrum argument, and to his claim that my replica contains all that matters to me regarding the future. He considers a case where my neurons are replaced not by artificially constructed duplicates, but by those of my twin, who is exactly similar to me down to the cellular level. So, since our brains are qualitatively identical, this identity will occur also on the psychological level, so such a transplant will not affect psychological continuity at all. Robinson argues that while it is plausible to say that I survive in a near-end case, in the far-end case it is *my twin* who survives, not me, since the operation constitutes a brain transplant, with his brain being relocated in my body. Since all this takes place with full retention of psychological continuity, then psychological continuity cannot be a criterion of personal identity. The crucial difference in Robinson's example is that the replacement neurons are not causally related to mine—in particular, they are not copied from mine. I will have more to say about these examples in Chapter 5.

MY DIVISION

Parfit offers another set of powerful arguments in support of Relation R. These are again based on situations that are presently beyond our practical capabilities, but which, he argues, could become a reality in the future. In the section entitled 'My Division' (p. 254), he considers a case involving identical twins *A* and *B,* who are seriously injured such that *A's* body is damaged beyond repair but his brain is still functioning normally, whereas *B* has a seriously damaged brain but is otherwise uninjured. Now, by both the Physical and Psychological Criteria, if *A's* brain were transplanted into B's body, the resulting person would be A, as the receipt of a new body can be seen more accurately as a limiting case of organ transplant. This highlights what is reckoned to be unique about the brain in matters of identity. If B had received A's heart, lungs, liver and kidneys, then the resulting person remains B; but if A's brain is transplanted, then the resulting person is A. In fact it is more accurate to say that it is A who is the *recipient* here, and not the donor.

Parfit now asks us to consider the fact that substantially less than a complete brain can support a full human consciousness. For instance a stroke victim can suffer the loss of function of an entire cerebral hemisphere, yet relearn the associated abilities to some extent by the other hemisphere restructuring its 'division of labor' and taking these functions over. Likewise, people have survived hemispherectomy with psychological continuity largely intact. Secondly, Parfit notes that a small percentage of people do not have the usual pronounced functional division whereby language-related functions are dominantly carried out by one particular hemisphere (usually the left). In 'My Division' he concentrates on one such person whose linguistic functions are performed with equal input from both cerebral hemispheres.

Now imagine a case involving identical infant triplets A, B, & C. In an accident scenario similar to before, A survives with a healthy brain but a seriously damaged body, while B and C are brain-damaged but otherwise uninjured. Realizing that if nothing is done all three will die, surgeons decide to cut their losses (excuse that dreadful pun). They remove and divide A's brain so that one cerebral hemisphere each is inserted into the empty skulls of B and C, their cortexes having been removed. So who survives? By analyzing the outcome in terms of the concept of personal identity, Parfit says that we have four possibilities:

1. A does not survive;
2. A survives as the B-body-person, and is identical with him;
3. A survives as the C-body-person, and is identical with him;
4. A survives as, and is identical with, both the B- and C-body-person.

He argues that each of these outcomes fails, and that such cases are much better analyzed in terms of Relation R.

Starting with 1, we have already accepted that A survives if his full brain is transplanted into B's body. Secondly, we've accepted that A would have survived with full (or sufficient) psychological continuity had he undergone a hemispherectomy. Combining these considerations, we must conclude that if *one* of A's cerebral hemispheres were transplanted into B's body, then the resulting person would be A. So, given all this, how could anything happening to A's *other* hemisphere affect this survival? If anything, we seem to have a 'double success,' with A surviving twice-over, contrary to what Nozick concludes.

Numbers 2 and 3 can be treated together, being two sides of the same coin. The problem is that since any argument in favor of one applies equally to the other, we can have no rational grounds for choosing one of these two outcomes over the other. This leaves us with 4. The problem here is that the result is contrary to the logic of the identity relation. Identity is strictly a 'one:one' relation, i.e., x *(t1)* can be a stage of the same enduring object as only *one* such stage y *(t2)*. Since identity is a transitive relation, then, if A = the B-body-person, and if A = the C-body-person, then it follows that the B- and C-body-persons are likewise identical. Obviously this is not a coherent option. It is nonsense to say that A survives as one person with a divided mind and two bodies. The problem is not that this would drastically distort our concept of a person. I have no objections in principle about that since I believe that the concept of 'person' is vague, and also, as Brennan argues, is capable of sustaining several incompatible developments. But this development is clearly a nonstarter. The B- and C-body-persons could be separated and never see nor hear from each other again, so the claim that they nevertheless constitute one person is worthless, adding nothing to our understanding of the situation.

John Robinson challenges Parfit's description of his thought-experiments, and his unstated assumption that the two cerebral hemispheres (or, as he puts it, the two 'half-brains') together constitute one whole brain. On similar grounds, he criticizes Parfit's description of hemispherectomy patients as having survived with 'half their brain destroyed,' since in such cases the *brainstem* must also be considered:

> *If we were to transplant the removed hemisphere into someone else's brainless body, we would not create a second person. It is only if we were to transplant the hemisphere into a body that already had some brain in it, the brainstem, that there would be another person as a result. Once this feature of the puzzle case is highlighted, then it becomes quite clear that the relation between a surviving subject before and after the removal of one of the hemispheres is not duplicated in the case where the surviving subject's hemisphere is removed and placed in someone else's skull. In the former case, but not the latter, there is the persisting brainstem to consider, and the psychological abilities and capacities that supervene on it* (p. 324).

Can Parfit defend himself against this criticism? Perhaps he could say something like this: while obviously granting that the brain comprises a number of highly interdependent sub-systems, where the functioning of each part depends on the integrity of the other parts, so that the possibility of conscious experience will depend on the functions of the brainstem, it is wrong to suggest that the brainstem is the bearer of any of the higher mental functions comprising psychological continuity. On the contrary, the functions of the brainstem operate below the level of conscious awareness, dealing with balance, control and movement. It would take a strong argument, which Robinson does not provide, to say why *these* functions should count regarding matters of identity any more than, say, the functions of cleansing the blood or of metabolizing fats. So when *A's* hemisphere is transplanted into *B's* skull, there is no reason to suggest that *B's* brainstem be granted any weight regarding the question of identity, any more than does *B*'s kidneys or liver. The resulting person is clearly *A*.

In reply to *this*, I have devised a thought-experiment that seems to count against Parfit, and adds to the chaos that is being brought about by the use of these fictions. Imagine that the Scottish Football Association, in a fit of desperation, has abducted both myself and the Argentinian genius Diego Maradona (if this example becomes outdated, substitute the player of your choice). A neurosurgeon performs a Parfitian brain-swap, whereby our respective cortexes are exchanged. Now Parfit and many others would be inclined to say that by both the Physical and Psychological Criteria, I would be the DM-body-person, who will spend his time pondering over weighty philosophical tomes, whilst the JB-body-person emerges with memories of the backstreets of Buenos Aires. However, the finely tuned balance and poise of a top class athlete are primarily within the domain not of the cortex, but of the cerebellum, which has not been transplanted. So, in justified disagreement with philosophical orthodoxy, the JB-body-person's coach would disagree that he was Maradona, if his skills remained at the mediocre level of your humble author. From the coach's perspective, the one who is identical with Maradona is whoever *plays* like Maradona, no matter what he does or doesn't remember.

One might respond that it is misleading to talk in this way, making such a clear-cut division between experience memory and procedural memory, in saying that one can be completely lost without the other being affected. However, as we shall see in Chapter 6, this is precisely the situation of some amnesiacs. One such person, Clive Wearing, has suffered a virtually complete loss of long-term experience memory, yet various practical skills, notably his ability to play the piano, have remained intact. Of course, he doesn't *know* that he can play until he actually does it. So perhaps it would be irrelevant that the DM-body-person would be dragged reluctantly from his books onto the field, protesting that he really wasn't very good, if these skills came alive once the game began.

Leaving these doubts aside for the moment, let us return to Parfit and 'My Division.' Since he has rejected all possible outcomes described in terms of identity, he argues that we are forced to recognize that the concept of identity is inadequate and inappropriate to describe what is going on in such cases. Even if we had all possible factual information regarding the operations, this would not enable us to settle questions of identity through time. Thus, he concludes, such questions are *empty.*

Consequently, it is irrational to regard such an operation as being 'as bad as death,' since the relationships between *A* and the *B*- and *C*-body-persons contain all that matters regarding survival, namely Relation R, psychological continuity by any means. The fact that Relation R does not take this 'branching' form in normal cases is of no concern, since branching does not alter the intrinsic quality of the relation. Nor does it contravene its logic, as Relation R need not be a one:one relation, unlike identity. Parfit suggests that we are led to the mistaken belief that personal identity is the one relation that contains all that matters regarding our survival because in all actual cases it coincides with Relation R. He regards the value of deploying these thought-experiments as being to show situations where the two relations diverge, and where we must choose between them.

THE 'ONLY X AND Y' RULE

Williams [1957] develops another argument against any Psychological Criterion. It arises out of a remark by Thomas Reid against Locke's claim that *"whosoever has the consciousness of the past and present actions is the same person to whom they belong."* To Reid, it seemed that *"if the same consciousness can be transferred from one intelligent being to another... then two or twenty intelligent beings may be the same person"* (p. 114). Williams begins by acknowledging the 'one:one' character of the identity relation, and thus that I cannot be identical with two future persons at any given time. Thus, if it were possible that two future persons were psychologically continuous with me, then psychological continuity cannot provide a criterion for the holding of personal identity, since a criterion for a 'one:one' relation must also take this form.

He adds that even if an advocate of the Psychological Criterion were to compromise and propose non-branching psychological continuity as a criterion, this will not do, because any criterion must satisfy two requirements (which, following Brennan, I have called the 'only *x* and *y* rule'). Firstly (as described earlier in this chapter) whether or not x $(t1)$ is the same person as y $(t2)$ must only depend on factors intrinsic to x and y—what happens to anyone else cannot affect the answer. Secondly, since identity is a matter of the utmost importance, this answer cannot depend on *trivial* matters.

So by a Lockean theory (to be discussed in detail in Chapter 6), if I were to wake up one morning with memories of Napoleon's life, then I would thereby *be* Napoleon. But, as Reid implies, it is no more implausible to suggest that if this can happen once, then it can happen any number of times. So, for example, if *you* were also to find yourself with these memories, then you too would be Napoleon. But we can't both be Napoleon, not just because the 'one:one' form of the identity relation is violated, but because it would follow from the transitivity of the identity relation that you and I would be identical, which we are not.

Parfit considers his Teletransporter case (to be discussed in Chapter 4) from the point of view of Williams' requirements.

I enter a machine that records the exact states of all my cells, and transmits this information to Mars, where it is used to create a qualitatively identical body. Psychological continuity is preserved, since the entire process takes place at the speed of light. My original body is simultaneously destroyed. According to a non-branching wide Psychological Criterion, I survive as my replica. But what if this information comprising my 'blueprint' were also sent to Io (a satellite of Jupiter) but stored there without producing another replica? By this criterion, I would only survive as the same person on Mars as long as no other replica were made. But no *intrinsic* change would be undergone by the Mars-replica on the creation of the Io-replica. The point is that the question of whether or not I survive on Mars cannot, by the 'only x and y' rule, depend on events on Io which involve someone else.

However, Parfit then hoists Williams with his own petard by using this argument to challenge the *Physical* Criterion. In fact he goes much further, arguing that *no* criterion can satisfy Williams' requirements in all possible cases. He devises another thought-experiment involving our hapless triplets A, B, and C, where A's cortex is removed and divided, with each hemisphere moved to a separate room for transplant into B and C's skulls. A supporter of a non-branching Physical Criterion would say that if one hemisphere were successfully transplanted into B's body, and the other operation were to fail, then A = the B-body-person; but that if the second operation had been successful, then A does not survive as either resulting person. But such a claim violates Williams' requirements, which rule that if A = the B-body-person, then this cannot be affected by anything that happens to the C-body-person. To claim otherwise is to allow a situation where, if there is a one-hour delay between the two operations, A survives as the B-body-person for one hour, until the first signs of neural activity in the C-body-person.

The only recourse for a defender of the Physical Criterion seems to be to modify it to rule out branching, e.g., by saying that x (t1) is identical with y (t2) if and only if y has a full human consciousness and more than half of x's brain. This criterion, suggested by Wiggins (1980), can only take a 'one:one' form, and thus satisfies the first of Williams' requirements. However, it fails the second. If we assume, in accordance with philosophical tradition, that by 'brain' Wiggins means 'cortex,' then possession of more than half a cortex is not a necessary condition of having a full human consciousness, as hemispherectomy patients demonstrate. Also, the tiny difference that may separate 'less than half a brain' from 'more than half a brain' (i.e., 49.99...9% v 50.00...1%) is *trivial,* if the two brains function equally well. Otherwise, we could have the situation of a hemispherectomy patient losing his identity (and not realizing the fact) if a tiny fraction of his remaining hemisphere were destroyed, without his mental capacities being affected.

Because of these considerations, Parfit says that neither the Physical nor the Psychological Criterion can meet Williams' requirements; and that such problems equally affect *any* potential criterion. However, he continues, the problems and paradoxes fall away if we examine the above mentioned cases in terms of Relation R. By turning from all talk of identity, then in 'My Division,' we don't bother asking if A is the same person as the B- or C- body-persons, but rather say that A is *R-related* to both. (This can be expressed as *ARB* & *ARC*.) In advocating this view, we would hold that such relationships contained all that was of any importance in the identity relation. Such revised theories can satisfy analogues of Williams' requirements, i.e., *ARB* no matter what happens to *C*, and despite any trivial event that might occur elsewhere. In any cases (which will be the overwhelming majority) that seem to suggest that identity is the only relation that can accommodate all that really matters regarding survival in the future, this will be because in each such case it coincides with Relation R.

APPENDIX: LEWIS—THE INDETERMINACY OF POPULATION

A far more radical solution to the problem of branching has been proposed by David Lewis, who has taken part in a long-standing debate with Parfit concerning survival and identity. I will argue that Lewis' theory has consequences that are so unattractive and counterintuitive that we ought to reject it.

Note: This section is difficult, and can be safely passed over. The debate is self-contained, and plays no part in the rest of the book.

Parfit (see [1971]) has long argued that what matters regarding the future, when viewed from the perspective of self-interest, is Relation R, and not necessarily that *I* survive, i.e., that there need not be some future person who is identical-through-time with me. He accepts that these two relations, identity and Relation R, have always coincided in practice. However, the dispute has focused on thought-experiments in which one person at *t1* has two persons at *t2* who have equally strong identity claims on him. For example, one popular scenario depicts someone entering a 'duplication machine' from which two people emerge, both being physically and psychologically exactly similar to the original person.

Such hypothetical cases are problematic due to the different logical structures of the two relations. As I have said, identity is a 'one:one' relation, i.e., *x (t1)* is identical through time with, at most, one *y (t2)*. However, Relation R is not thus constrained, and can also take 'one:many' or 'many:one' forms (of 'fission' or 'fusion' respectively). If such cases do occur, it seems that the identity relation is inadequate to pronounce on the results. As the previous sections have described, Parfit uses 'fission' cases to separate the two relations, and to argue that in a case in which psychological continuity is maintained but in which I do not survive, the result is still as good as 'ordinary' survival. Thus in normal cases in which the two relations coincide, the identity relation is merely a passenger, as Relation R contains all that matters regarding future survival.

Lewis's response [1976] is to agree that what matters regarding the future is the holding of Relation R. But he also claims firstly that what matters is the holding of identity through time, and secondly that there is no contradiction in claiming that both matter, since the formal discrepancy between them only shows that they are *different* relations, not that they are mutually exclusive. Lewis rightly points out that identity and Relation R have different relata. Relation R is a relation between momentary *person-stages,* whereas identity is applied to continuant *persons* who have different stages. Identity does not hold between person-stages as, by definition, no stage will survive in the future.

However, according to Lewis, another relation can be derived from identity, one which, like Relation R, does hold between person-stages. This is what he calls the *'I-relation,'* which holds between all stages of a single continuant person. Since they share the same relata, *this* is the relation that should be compared to Relation R in judging whether Parfit is correct to say that Relation R, not identity, contains all that matters to future survival. Lewis argues that if what matters is the holding of identity, then this corresponds to the claim that one's present person-stage is I-related to future person-stages. He then goes on to claim that in all *possible* cases, any stage is I-related and R-related to exactly the same set of stages. Therefore, since they are necessarily coextensive, *the I-relation = Relation R.* Thus there is no incompatibility in saying that both identity and Relation R are what matter in survival.

We can thereby derive a non-circular definition of a person in terms of Relation R. Since a person is a maximal I-interrelated aggregate of stages (i.e., each stage is I-related to all other stages and to itself, and since a person is not part of any larger I-related aggregate), then, since the I-relation = Relation R, then a person can be defined as a maximal R-interrelated aggregate of person-stages.

Let us now return to the hypothetical case in which Relation R takes a 'branching' form, i.e., where one stage is R-related to stages that are not R-related to each other. Let the single pre-fission stage be called '*S*', and the two concurrent post-fission stages be called '*S1*' and '*S2*.' In such a situation, *S* is R-related to *S1* and to *S2*, but *S1* and *S2* are not R-related to each other. Such a case seems to show that Relation R is intransitive and, since identity is a transitive relation, then in such cases we will have to choose between the two relations regarding which contains all that matters in survival.

Lewis responds to this challenge by saying that while identity is a transitive relation, the I-relation need not be, and that in fission cases the I-relation will display relationships between stages that parallel those of Relation R. So *S* is I-related to *S1* and to *S2*, but *S1* and *S2* are not I-related to each other. Lewis permits this state of affairs as he conceives such cases as involving a partial *overlap* between continuant persons. Thus if we say that *S* occurs at *t1*, and that *S1* and *S2* occur at *t2*, then *S* is *shared* by two distinct persons *C1* and *C2*, where *S1* is a stage of *C1* and not of *C2*, and where *S2* is a stage of *C2* and not of *C1*.

So in order to sustain his identification of the relations I and R, Lewis is committed to the claim that two (or, in theory, more) persons can share the same person-stage, and therefore that fission is not a case of one person resulting in two persons, as there were two people there all along. As he admits, such an overlap leads to 'over-population' since, in counting a population or any subset thereof (e.g., 'the number of people in room *A* at *t1*'), we can either count the number of *people* having stages at *t1*, or we can count the number of stages themselves. Now obviously in a world in which no such overlap takes place (e.g., the real world) both methods of counting will always deliver the same answer. However if cases of overlap do occur, then there will be a discrepancy, with there being more persons than person-stages present.

Having reached this position, and possibly to avoid its counterintuitiveness, Lewis changes tack, arguing that we needn't do our counting by using the relation of identity, but can rather employ the relation of *'tensed identity'* or 'identity-at-*t*,' wherein *x* and *y* are identical-at-*t* if and only if both *x* and *y* exist at *t*, and their stages at *t* are identical. Tensed identity is not a relation holding between stages, but a relation between continuants that derives from a relation between stages. Yet unlike identity per se it is not a relation of identity between continuants, but a weaker relation with properties of equivalence and indiscernibility for the class of properties logically determined by the properties of the person's stage at *t*. So in a fission case where branching occurred at *t2*, then counting with the relation of identity-at-*t1* (i.e., before fission) there was *one* person present, but by counting with the relation of identity-at-*t2* there were *two*.

Parfit [1976] challenged Lewis' parallels between the I and R relations in fission cases, arguing that they cannot support his compatibilist position regarding identity and Relation R over what matters in survival. By Lewis' description of the above case in terms of two persons *C1* and *C2*, *C1's* stage *S* is R-related to *C2's* stage *S2*. But since *C1* and *C2* are different persons, and thus *C1* stands in the relation that matters (Relation R) to *someone else*, how then can the relation that matters either be or be compatible with identity? Parallel with *S* being R-related to *S2*, Lewis holds that *S* is I-related to *S2*. But surely if we thereby have *C1's* stage *S*, and *C2's* stage *S2*, as being stages of the same person, then surely it is the *wrong* person, namely *C2*. Lewis wants to say that both identity and Relation R satisfy conditions on 'what matters' regarding survival. Now, given that *S* is R-related to *S2*, then *S2* stands to *C1* in the relation that matters to *C1's* survival. Yet if he also wants to say that identity is the relation that matters, he needs to show that both *S* and *S2* are stages of *C1*, and, since *S2* is not, his argument fails.

Lewis, in a postscript to his original article [1983], attempts to counter Parfit's objections by considering a case in which at stage *S*, before fission but after *C1* and *C2* are informed of their imminent division, there is a desire for survival *"of the most common-sensical and unphilosophical kind possible,"* and, since *S* is a shared stage, this desire is a shared one between *C1* and *C2*. Now if it turns out that *C1* dies shortly after fission, and *C2* continues to live for a considerable time, then *C2* clearly has his pre-fission wish for survival satisfied. But does *C1?* Is Parfit not right in saying that from *C1's* point of view regarding identity, *C2* is the *wrong person?*

Lewis replies that this would only be the case if *C1's* desire was that he, *C1,* survived. But this was not the most straightforward desire that could have occurred, which is rather 'let *us* survive,' or 'let at least one of us survive.' Thus, on this model, *C1's* desire for survival *is* satisfied. Lewis adds that in cases where *C1* and *C2* don't know about their imminent fission, then the singular desire 'let *me* survive' can be thought or uttered, but is unsatisfiable since it rests on the false assumption that there is a 'me,' one single person there.

So Lewis offers us a choice. Either we count persons by the relation of identity, with the result that in cases of fission there were two persons all along prior to their splitting. Or we can count by the relation of 'tensed identity,' which produces results more in line with our intuitions. Taking these two proposals in turn, I find the first option by far the less plausible, as it leads to problems that reduce it to absurdity. Let us take a basic case of fission in which one person at *t1* results in two persons at *t2*. When I want to indicate their plurality, I will call these persons *C1* and *C2*. When I want to be neutral regarding the question of how many persons share the same pre-fission stages, I shall simply refer to *C.* Now contrast the position of *C* with that of any *other* two persons who might be present, *D* and *E,* who are not subject to fission at any future time. Lewis must accept that *D* and *E* are 'different persons,' to each other at *t1* in vastly different ways than are *C1* and *C2* at *t1.* They have different bodies, different mental states, and generally can be clearly distinguished and individuated at *t1,* whereas *C1* and *C2* clearly can not. When asked exactly *how C1* and *C2* are different persons, Lewis will reply that they are two different people sharing a set of stages. But when he is asked to explicate or to justify this claim, he can only talk in terms of their future fission—but nothing is thereby explained.

There is nothing intrinsic to C, either physically or psychologically, that could betray any difference at $t1$ between C and other, singular, persons such as D and E in such a way as to reveal his plurality. In a world in which fission occurs, there is no way of telling at $t1$, or indeed at *any* given time, just how many people are present within a given space. Since the number of people present isn't necessarily the same as the number of person-stages (which will be individuated by a physical criterion, by counting bodies), we are left with a question that is unanswerable *in principle,* which should lead us to suspect that it is not a legitimate question at all, and that the theory within which the question is grounded is incoherent.

Over and above these epistemological problems, there is the deeper issue that the very matter of the number of persons present at a given time will depend on the number of fissions that occur at later times. In other words, the number of persons present at $t1$ will be a function of events at $t2$, $t3$, etc. To bring out the absurdity of this position, let us consider a couple of hypothetical examples.

C is sitting in the duplication machine at $t1$. The switch that activates the creation of a duplicate is to be pressed at $t2$. However, the machine is a little unreliable due to bad wiring. Sometimes it works, sometimes not. By Lewis' theory, if the machine works at $t2$, then there were two persons sitting in it at $t1$; whereas if it is out of order at $t2$, then there was only one there at $t1$.

Now imagine that C is sitting in a new 'superduplicator' which can produce any number of 'copies' at the rate of one per minute. It would follow that the question of the number of persons present in the machine at $t1$ would not admit of a determinate answer, as this number would be rising at the rate of one per minute with, in principle, no upper limit. Given that Lewis can't provide a criterion for counting the number of persons present at any time, how can he even have any real grasp of the concept of 'person'?

I now turn to the option of counting by the relation of tensed identity. I have no objections to such a device, but I take a different lesson from Lewis' to resort to its usage. Lewis seems to think that the fact that fission cases can be described in terms of such a relation gives support to his main thesis that identity and Relation R provide compatible answers to the question of what matters in survival. I, on the contrary, note that 'identity-at-t' is a different relation to identity per se, and is irreducible to it. Thus, resorting to the use of this new relation only confirms Parfit's argument that the logic of the identity relation prevents it from adequately describing fission cases, whereas Relation R is clearly up to the task. If such cases actually occurred, e.g., if a duplication machine were ever invented, then presumably there would be a satisfactory theory of how the process took place, and the concepts involved in this explanation would constitute the language in which fission cases would be completely described. So any further questions regarding the identity of the pre- and post-fission persons would be empty.

CHAPTER THREE

ASPECTS OF NON-REDUCTIONISM

This chapter falls into three main parts. In the first part (up to page 43) I will consider Joseph Butler's argument that the Psychological Criterion is question-begging. After various interpretations and extensions of Butler's argument, I will introduce the concept of 'quasi-memory.' The second part is devoted to a discussion of the ideas of Richard Swinburne, who is probably the leading contemporary Non-Reductionist. Finally, in the third part I cast a skeptical eye over claims that parapsychology might provide grounds for Non-Reductionism.

BUTLER'S CHARGE OF CIRCULARITY

Contemporary versions of the Psychological Criterion can be traced back to John Locke [1694]. Any such criterion must face up to the charge of circularity, as originally proposed by Joseph Butler [1736]. This charge has been remarkably resilient, and I put its survival down to the fact that it is unclear which point Butler is trying to make. I will consider various interpretations and extensions deriving from Butler, and argue that the Psychological Criterion can survive attacks from all of them.

I will begin with Butler's classic statement that "one should really think it self-evident that consciousness of personal identity presupposes, and therefore cannot constitute personal identity any more than knowledge, in any other case, can constitute truth, which it presupposes" (p. 100). Basically, Butler is saying that the holding of personal identity cannot consist in the existence of states of con-sciousness, nor in any relations between mental states, as these can only discover that the identity relation holds. But this discovery can be made only if the identity is already there to be discovered. Therefore the Psychological Criterion already presupposes the exis-tence of the identity that it claims to constitute. Butler goes on to say that personal identity is indefinable and irreducible, and that any attempt to define it will fail: "Now, when it is asked wherein personal identity consists, the answer should be the same as if it were asked, wherein consists similitude or equality; that all attempts to define, would but perplex it" (p. 99).

One aspect of Butler's position is to deny that a direct present awareness of one's identity can be constitutive of it, since the awareness presupposes the identity. In other words, Butler can be read as attributing to Locke the Cartesian doctrine that the self is directly revealed in the act of introspection, but as then pointing out that such an act can only discover, but not constitute, such a self. The immediate retort to Butler comes with Hume's famous insight that introspection never reveals 'oneself,' but only one's mental states:

For my part, when I enter most intimately into what I call myself, I always stumble on some particular perception or other, of heat or cold, light or shade, love or hatred, pain or pleasure. I can never catch myself at any time without a perception, and can never observe any thing but the per-ception (1739, Book I, Part IV, section 6).

Butler also falls into another deep error. His argument is an instanti-ation of an implicit general claim that a direct perception or experi-ence of x presupposes the prior existence of x independently of this awareness of it, and therefore cannot be constitutive of it. But there are counterexamples to this rule. For instance, one cannot say that the experience of pain cannot constitute pain but can only discover it because this presupposes a pain already there to be aware of. Such an argument is obviously wrong since there is no more to a pain than the experience of pain. To think otherwise is to reify the pain and drive a wedge between the 'thing' itself and the experience of it. This is what Butler (on this interpretation) has done to the self. In his defense, he is only highlighting an issue that Locke never resolved.

Butler is clearly committed to a view of the self as a thing, a substance, a *res cogitans*. But it is due to the unique nature of such a purported substance that Butler's thesis that 'knowledge of x presupposes the truth of x' is not applicable to it. Unlike a case where, for example, the act of perceiving a car presupposes a car already there to be seen, the act of perceiving a Cartesian Ego in introspection would consist of the very act of the self perceiving itself, which would be an irreducibly reflexive act. So such an observer would not merely be discovering such a self, but would by this very act be manifesting its essential nature. Thus such an act would be constitutive of the self and of personal identity, if such a substance existed (which, I suggest, it does not).

The other strand of Butler's position is to take Locke's claim that one's identity is revealed by one's memories of past experiences, but to point out again that such a discovery presupposes the existence of that which is discovered. The trouble this time is that 'being the same person at the present time $t2$ as the person who experienced event e at some past time $t1$' is not a possible content of a memory. This is of a different logical type to anything that could be a possible memory—in other words, this is not a past experience. My point is parallel to Ayer's strengthening of Hume's attack on the notion of a direct acquaintance with the self, whereby it is not just a matter of fact that when I examine the contents of my consciousness I can only perceive a succession of perceptions. It is rather a matter of logic, as such a 'self' is not a logically possible content of experience. Now if this point is true of the present tense, then it is equally true of the past tense, regarding memories of such experiences of the self. If the self cannot be experienced in the first place, then it cannot be remembered.

So on either of my two readings of Butler, Locke may be guilty of many things, but they do not include circularity. The factor that distinguishes a genuine memory isn't the circular condition that the memory is *mine,* but that there is a causal connection between the original experience and the subsequent memory of it, whereby the experience of *e* causes a memory trace to be stored in the brain that can be brought into conscious awareness at a later date as a 'memory of *e*.' (These issues are the topic of Chapter 6.)

QUASI-MEMORY

Perhaps the charge of circularity can be formulated in another way. One might argue that memory cannot provide a criterion for personal identity because it is part of the conditions of use of the concept of memory that one can only remember one's own experiences. In other words, the statement 'I remember experiencing *e* at *t*' is elliptical for 'I remember *my* experiencing *e* at *t*.' This claim can be supported by Gareth Evans' remarks regarding the 'identification-free' nature of memory-judgments. In other words, while I can be mistaken about the *content* of a memory, or regarding whether it is a real memory rather than just a product of imagination, I cannot be mistaken about whether or not it is *mine*. As Evans says:

"Memory is not a way of possessing knowledge about an object of a kind which leaves open the question of the identity of that object. If a subject has, in virtue of the operation of his memory, knowledge of the past states of a subject, then that subject is himself" (p. 245).

However, taking this analysis of memory-judgments seriously has a crippling effect on inquiries into personal identity. For example, speculation about the possibility of my remembering your experiences through a transplant of specific neural structures would, like many thought-experiments, be ruled out by linguistic convention. This might appear to be throwing the baby out with the bathwater. On the other hand, one person's category mistake is often another person's need for conceptual revision. So perhaps we are justified in trampling over linguistic niceties, if our speculations pay off in greater understanding of self and identity.

In a similar spirit, Parfit introduces the concept of 'quasi-memory,' which is defined so to be free of the suspicion of circularity. I have a quasi-memory of some experience *e* if and only if

1. I seem to remember having *e;*
2. Someone had *e;*
3. My apparent memory is causally dependent, in the right sort of way, on this past experience of *e*.

At this point, Non-Reductionists will respond that Parfit cannot spell out restrictions on what would count as 'the right kind of cause' in 3 without invoking personal identity (i.e., by requiring that *e* is *my* experience) and that the analysis is therefore circular. Such an argument is mistaken. The whole force of a memory-based criterion lies in the fact that memory is a causal process. As I have noted, in the normal case an experience is encoded in the brain and stored as a memory trace. Now the claim that I could only quasi-remember my own experiences assumes that this is the only causal means whereby experiences could be recalled. However, if memory traces could be transferred from one brain to another, for instance, if the memory trace of *e* were transferred from *A's* brain into *B's* brain, then *B* would be capable of having true quasi-memories of *e*.

So we do have conceivable examples of an appropriate causal connection holding between mental states without the experiencer and the rememberer being the same person. Cases of fission would provide other examples. In fact, in such hypothetical circumstances it would be possible to identify a causal connection between an experience and a quasi-memory prior to the establishment of facts regarding identity. Consider a case of brain transfer. If *B* has quasi-memories at *t2* of *A's* experiences at *t1*, then the fact that he has the same brain at *t2* that *A* had at *t1* itself provides sufficient reason for saying that the quasi-memories were appropriately caused, and this in turn provides sufficient grounds for saying that *A* = *B*.

Parfit goes on to say that he would accept *any* sufficient cause as 'the right kind of cause' to allow quasi-memory. I agree, and would add that any such cause would be accepted once we had some understanding of the processes that would enable quasi-memories to take place. For example, in the case of a memory-trace transplant, such an operation would be performed against the background of a neurologically based theory of memory. We would thus have knowledge of a cluster of laws underlying the process, which would ensure regularity so that predictions could be made regarding y remembering e if x's neural net N (which stored the memory) was implanted in y's brain. Conversely, the occurrence of such a quasi-memory could be explained by such a theory.

No doubt if such events ever became commonplace, then our common set of attitudes regarding memory would gradually change so that it would cease to be part of our concept of memory that we could only remember our own experiences. In other words, our concept of memory would gradually involve into the concept of quasi-memory. It would just be that the old, 'natural' means of remembering could be described in terms of the functioning of a single brain.

Of course, these thought-experiments may be impossible in principle. But this is an empirical matter, confirmable only in the event of such neural transplants taking place. But for the sake of argument, let us be charitable and allow for the moment that memories can be thus transferred. Parfit constructs such an example in which someone could be plausibly said to have true quasi-memories of someone else's experiences. Imagine that a neurosurgeon has implanted copies of certain of Paul's memory traces into Jane's brain, so that she seems to remember events happening in Venice, a city that she knows she has never visited. However, she knows that Paul has been there, and he confirms that her states correspond to certain of his experiences while in Venice. Jane can conclude that she is quasi-remembering one of Paul's experiences. We can even imagine Paul 'testing' Jane in order to distinguish genuine recollection from mere imagination. It might go something like this: "Well, Jane, so you remember being in a gondola, and catching sight of a small, red-coated figure in an alleyway... what happened next?"

There could also be cases where Jane could work out for herself whether something was a memory of her own life, or a quasi-memory from Paul's life. Parfit gives such an example, where Jane recalls shaving and seeing Paul's reflection in the mirror instead of her own. The significance of this example lies in its being of an experience in which one is actively physically involved, and where one's perception of one's body plays an integral role in the action, and will therefore be likewise 'featured' in the corresponding memories or quasi-memories.

It is worth noticing that it is not always the case that 'oneself' enters into a memory as part of the content of a remembered event. As the above example illustrates, whether or not this happens depends on the extent of one's physical involvement in the event. So, for example, when I recall attending my first high school dance, I can 'see myself there' with clumsy movements, awkward conversation, pounding heart and clammy hands. When I remember this ordeal, *I* am the focus of the memory. On the other hand, we can acknowledge the power of a great performance or work of art to make the spectator 'forget himself' or 'lose the sense of himself.' So when I remember seeing a favorite movie, or a memorable concert or soccer game, I recall what happened on the screen, stage, or field. *I* am not present in the memory, and only reemerge when I recall the performance coming to an end. Before that, my only contribution is that of a transparent 'point of view.'

So, returning to Jane and Paul, she will have quasi-memories that will not be immediately identifiable as such, since neither she nor Paul will feature in the content of the purported memory. Such an experience will be recalled as being, in Parfit's words, 'from the seer's point of view.' There will be a conditional agnosticism regarding the identity of the subject of the original experience, tempered by the possibility that later evidence might appear that would indicate the subject.

SWINBURNE'S SIMPLE VIEW

Richard Swinburne is virtually unique among contemporary philosophers in attacking Reductionism from the perspective of dualism. He describes himself as adhering to the 'Simple View' regarding personal identity, namely in his agreement with Butler that it consists in some basic fact that is not reducible to any other facts concerning physical and/or psychological continuity. The Simple View holds that questions regarding identity have determinate answers in all possible cases, whether or not we can discover these answers. (Thus it is a form of Non-Reductionism.) Swinburne argues that to think otherwise is to fall into the fallacy of verificationism, of failing to distinguish the question of what counts as *evidence* for the holding of personal identity, from the question of what identity *consists in,* and thus of what it *means* to say that the relation holds. Thus he describes all forms of Reductionism (also known as the 'Complex View') as *empiricist* theories.

Clearly an empiricist theory will not suffice for someone who holds that all questions regarding personal identity must have a determinate answer since, as we have seen, there are a number of 'puzzle cases' to which no possible evidence can derive an answer, and thus any such answer would have to be found beyond the realm of empirical knowledge. In arguing that all Reductionist theories commit the verificationist fallacy, Swinburne, in the original statement of his views [1974], backs up his claim by reference to other examples of this fallacy that are, contrary to his assumption, far from analogous, as Madell points out. For example, in contrast to the problem of other minds, there is no such distinction between grounds for belief between first-person and third-person talk as, unlike this latter case, no one is saying that only talk of others' identity transcends all possible evidence that I could have. The debate is about all cases, including one's own. Swinburne's second supposedly analogous case concerns our belief in the external world. However, this constitutes an explanatory hypothesis that best accounts for the regularities of sense-experience, whereas the positing of some 'self' over and above the body and the holding of physical and psychological continuity has no such role, being unnecessary to account for the comprehensibility of experience for an embodied object.

One way into the Simple View is to consider Swinburne's thought-experiment in which I am told that my brain (to be more precise, he should say my cerebral cortex) is to be removed, and the hemispheres separated, one each being transplanted into the cortexless skulls of bodies B and C. (Let us call me 'A'.) After these operations, one of the resulting persons, the B- or C-body-person, is to be tortured while the other is to be rewarded, à la Williams. It is up to me, A, to decide who is to get what, prior to the operations taking place.

Swinburne says that according to the Complex View it should make no difference to me either way as to who gets tortured and who is rewarded, as:

each person will be you to the extent that he has your brain and resembles you in his apparent memories and character... both subsequent persons will be part you... [and you will]... in part suffer and in part enjoy what each suffers and enjoys... [but] how could you have reason for part enjoyment and part terrified anticipation, when no one future person is going to suffer a mixed fate? (p. 18)

In this final sentence, Swinburne seems to be pointing to the intransitivity that such 'branching' results in, and is implying that since $B \neq C$, then $-[(A = B)$ & $(A = C)]$. Quite correct—however, in the above quotation, Swinburne makes his case at the cost of distorting his opponents' argument. A Reductionist like Parfit is not saying that under such circumstances, A is the same person as B and/or C to any extent, but rather that A *survives* as the B-body-person and as the C-body-person, as he is psychologically continuous (i.e. in Relation R) to both of them. In other words, this would be a case of survival without identity. Thus it seems reasonable to say that, faced with the thought of his future fission, $A's$ mixed feelings are well-justified, not because he nor any one future person will experience such mixed fortunes, but because he stands in Relation R to two different future persons, whose combined experience will encompass both the torture and the reward. In other words, in fission, stages $S2$ and $S3$ are R-related to a common earlier stage $S1$, but are not R-related to each other.

Swinburne goes on to say that we can make sense of the idea of A making the 'wrong choice,' i.e., of finding out that he is being tortured, or conversely of making the right choice, whereas by

Parfit's theory there is no real difference between the choices from *A's* perspective, and therefore no *risk*. Now it seems to me that we can only make sense of making a right or a wrong choice on the *assumption* that personal identity involves something beyond the physical and psychological continuities relating *A* & *B* and *A* & *C*, and thus such intuitions *cannot* non-question-beggingly be put forward as grounds in favor of the Simple View. If, on the other hand, there is no such 'further fact' that identity consists in, then we cannot make sense of there being a risk involved in the choice, as there is nothing left to be at stake.

Swinburne's response to *A's* dilemma is to say that there is equal *evidence* for the claims that *A* = *B* and that *A* = *C*, but that all such evidence is fallible, and the *fact* regarding which of *B* and *C* is identical with *A* is independent of such evidence. But, as I have mentioned, Parfit's line is somewhat different from that depicted by Swinburne. It is rather to say that certainly we cannot decide on all the possible evidence whether *A* = *B* or if *A* = *C*, and obviously *A* cannot be identical with *both*, so the problem is insoluble, and the question is empty. However, the situation can be re-described in terms of Relation R, and thus we can say that *A* survives equally in or as *B* and *C*.

Swinburne remarks that Reductionism's weakness in dealing with fission cases is in assuming that:

mere logic could determine which of the experiences had by various persons, each of which was to some extent continuous with me in apparent memory and brain matter, would be mine (p. 20),

whereas by the Simple View there being mine is a further fact, over and above any evidential considerations.

However, yet again he distorts the opposing position. Firstly, as I have mentioned, the Complex View needn't be cast in terms of which future experiences will be *mine*, and secondly, as Shoemaker [1984] says, the Complex View doesn't rely on 'mere logic,' but states that in cases in which answers to questions regarding identity *can* be given (which isn't always), then these answers will be ascertained on the basis of empirical *facts* regarding the causal relations between experiences, and that is all that there is to be said on the matter.

NON-REDUCTIONISM AND DUALISM

I will now turn to the matter of Swinburne's dualism and its relation to the Simple View. Looking at the components of the Simple View, it is clear that dualism cannot be derived from the indefinability or irreducibility of personal identity since, as Shoemaker notes, when terms refer to structured wholes, e.g., trees, cars, etc., one can hold that these terms are not reducible to, not definable in terms of the sum of their parts, but no one would want to therefore hold a dualist account of these.

Secondly, regarding the determinateness of questions of personal identity, Swinburne is mistaken to hold that any opposition to his theory must be based on verificationism. As Parfit points out, one can deny that all such questions regarding the identity of nations, clubs, etc. must yield a determinate answer, yet this denial isn't based on verificationist grounds. Thus further argument is required to show why the situation is in any way different in the case of persons. Rather, the denial that all identity-questions must admit of a determinate answer is due to vagueness in the sortal concept involved, namely 'person.' This vagueness allows an indeterminacy in the reference of items falling under such a concept, which in turn results in the indeterminacy of truth values of statements involving such referring terms.

Turning to another set of arguments, Swinburne seems to think that the truth of a dualist theory follows from the fact that he can, coherently and without contradiction, imagine that he could continue to exist in a disembodied state, being:

> able to operate on, and learn about the world... without having to use a particular chunk of matter for this purpose... [where]... simply by choosing to do so, he can gradually shift the focus of his knowledge and control (p. 24).

He accepts that such a disembodied existence would be impossible for a purely physical being, so, given that he's shown that it is logically possible, this must be due to the truth of what he calls his 'wider Aristotelian principle,' involving nonmaterial stuff organized into a certain form.

To begin with, I would dispute Swinburne's claim that the idea of disembodied existence is coherent. Imagination is a very deceptive faculty, rendering plausibility where it is not warranted. Certainly there is no blatant inconsistency in the way Swinburne describes it, but this is only because he offers such a fragmentary sketch. If he were to attempt to fill out a description of how disembodied existence was possible then it would be a different story, as he would then be required to account for how it is possible that one could perceive the world without sensory organs, or act upon the world without any muscles, etc., and it seems to me that there is no way in which these questions can be answered. Also, I'm not convinced that one *can* imagine being disembodied, in the sense of being able to grasp 'what it's like' from a subjective viewpoint, without tacitly introducing some elements of the physicality that is being denied. Speaking personally, I can just about imagine being invisible, or of being unable to feel my body, or being weightless, but that's as far as it goes.

On a more serious note, Swinburne's argument is not logically sound. As Shoemaker argues, Swinburne's claims that one might survive disembodied do not constitute a *de re* claim that, regarding one particular person, it is possible that *he* might survive in a disembodied state. At most it says that it is possible that there be some person that could do so. Yet Swinburne goes from this lesser claim to the realm of the actual, saying that "for any person who is presently conscious, there is no logical impossibility... that that person continue to exist without his body" (p. 29), which does not follow.

Neither does it follow from my being able to imagine myself as disembodied that such a state is a *de re* possibility for me. Arnauld had long ago dismissed such an argument from Descartes using a parallel case whereby I might doubt that a right-angled triangle has the property of having the square of its hypoteneuse equal to the sum of the squares of the other two sides. Clearly it does not follow that such a triangle does lack this property. Nor does it follow that the property is not an essential property of such a triangle. Likewise it may be that, despite my imagining in my ignorance that I could exist without a body, I am an essentially embodied being.

Next, Swinburne claims that 'laws of nature' do not necessitate that a certain person has certain memories nor that his body is made of certain matter. He imagines a time 4000 million years ago, when the earth was a cooling globe of inanimate chaos, and argues that while natural laws would dictate the general evolution of the planet and of the life-forms upon it, including the ways in which bodies would be formed that could support conscious life:

what natural laws in no way determine is <u>which</u> animate body is yours and which is mine... just the same arrangement of matter and just the same laws could have given me the body (and so the apparent memories) which are yours, and you the body (and so the apparent memories) which are now mine (p. 25–6).

However, yet again this argument presupposes what it sets out to prove. It assumes that there is a 'me' and a 'you' prior to the existence of the bodies we now 'occupy,' so that somehow I am allotted one such body, and you another. In other words, Swinburne again assumes the dualist theory, and the existence of immaterial souls prior to the existence of physical bodies.

THE SUBJECTIVE VIEW

I will finally turn now to another of Swinburne's arguments for the Simple View, wherein he claims that the ultimate irreducible nature of personal identity is proved from the fact that it is revealed in experience, and that no other theory can account for the co-personal relation (i.e., whereby they are all had by the same person) between experiences. He claims:

The continued existence of a person over a very short period of time is something that can often be experienced by that person...without it depending on our knowledge of anything more ultimate...the continuing of a person is a datum of experience (p. 41).

When we are tracking a moving object, it is an incomplete account of our experience to say that we see it at place *p1,* then at *p2, p3,* etc., as such perceptions do not come in discrete units, but *overlap* into one continuous awareness over time. He quotes Foster:

It is this double overlap which provides the sensible continuity of sense-experience and unified presentations into a stream of awareness...It is in the unity of the stream that we primarily discern the unity of the subject (p. 176).

Likewise, claims Swinburne, also among the data of our experience is the experience of oneself as being the common subject of simultaneous experiences, which are perceived as being 'mine' in a direct, non-inferential way, as this knowledge cannot be derived from any information regarding the experiences themselves, nor from knowledge regarding their associated brain-states.

On this set of arguments, I am in agreement with Shoemaker that one can go along with these observations concerning 'first-person knowledge,' but that such admissions leave the whole debate between the Simple and Complex Views untouched. It is certainly true that such instances of self-knowledge have the property of being immune from error due to misidentification, and it is a form of knowledge that is immediate and direct, and not derivable from any other information. However, we can hold that it is just a fact about the way in which human beings are constructed that being in a certain state or having a certain experience directly causes the incorrigible belief that I am in such a state or am having the experience. But this does not imply that personal identity cannot be given a non-circular and substantial definition in terms of other relations.

Also, as Shoemaker observes, Swinburne has yet to offer any argument to suggest that a dualist theory would provide any insights into the peculiar properties of self-knowledge. Merely saying that it consists in an unanalyzable fact has no explanatory power at all.

The final blow to Swinburne comes when we recall the standard objections to dualism, namely of accounting for how two mutually distinct substances could causally interact, and secondly how a criterion of identity for minds could be devised that does not depend on some physical criterion. Swinburne does not acknowledge these problems, let alone try to solve them.

EMPIRICAL GROUNDS FOR NON-REDUCTIONISM?

In Section 82 of *Reasons and Persons,* Parfit ignores the contemporary wisdom that the Cartesian Ego is an incoherent concept, and makes the surprising concession that it is just a contingent fact that no such entities exist. He then suggests the kind of evidence that would justify the belief that such units of non-material substance could exist as separate entities. Such evidence would prove the truth of Non-Reductionism, the theory that persons consist of more than a body and brain and sets of mental and physical states, and that the holding of personal identity is a further fact that is irreducible to any facts concerning these.

He offers an example that would provide proof of reincarnation. He considers the imaginary case of a modern-day Japanese woman who experiences what seem to be memories of having lived many thousands of years ago as a Celtic warrior. On the basis of these quasi-memories, she makes predictions concerning the discovery of certain archeological artifacts, which are later confirmed. Parfit says that, if

1. there actually were many well-confirmed cases like this; and
2. there were no other ways of accounting for such detailed and specific knowledge of the past,

we would have to concede that quasi-memories of past lives are possible. Given the absence of physical continuity between the alleged person having the original experiences and the person remembering them, we would seem to be obliged to posit the existence of a purely mental entity that extended through time to cover both embodiments, i.e., throughout the thousands of years separating the Celtic and Japanese-bodied persons. In such a case, we would have strong grounds for saying that this non-material entity would be the essential bearer of personhood, such that the lifetimes of the Celtic warrior and the Japanese woman would be two sets of stages of the life of one and the same person. The only trouble, says Parfit, is that no such cases really exist, and thus we have no evidence for the existence of such non-material entities. In other words, there are no such empirical grounds for Non-Reductionism.

So let us consider the type of evidence that Parfit is referring to. Go into any bookstore and you will find a number of books in which someone is claiming to have led an interesting life in ancient Egypt, or to be in contact with Elvis, or to be 'channelling' warnings about some imminent apocalypse from a spirit guide. To the horror of all philosophers, these tend to be placed in a section marked 'Metaphysics.' I, like many people, have a hard time taking any of this material seriously. However, my rejection of the paranormal goes beyond Parfit's mere denial of its veracity. It is rather that even if such reports were true, this alone provides no grounds for Non-Reductionism, since what is required, and not provided, is a Non-Reductionist *explanation* of what is going on in such cases.

So, for the sake of argument, let us pretend that some of these reports of paranormal events are true. Recall that Parfit stipulated that for such evidence to justify Non-Reductionism, there had to be no other explanations of such phenomena available. I am saying that there are no explanations available *at all*. For example, suppose that someone claimed that ESP provided the type of explanation we are looking for. The idea is that information is taken to be derived:

1. telepathically from living people who are informed of the given facts;
2. by retrospective clairvoyant observation of the events in question;
3. by clairvoyant observation of existing records or circumstantial evidence of these events.

Supporters of ESP regard it as the most economical hypothesis as it only relies on purported capacities of the mind, and doesn't invoke problematic entities such as disembodied souls. However, ESP cannot cover *all* cases of paranormal cognition without attributing a virtually unlimited range of powers to the persons con-

cerned. In fact, the explanatory force of the ESP hypothesis is minimal, since there isn't the slightest suggestion of *how* the mind can
acquire the knowledge concerned. In the absence of any acceptable
theory of the process of knowledge acquisition, the claim that the
mind acquires this information through ESP is akin to the fallacy
of saying that opium makes you sleep due to its 'dormative virtue.'

So, if any such paranormal events have actually occurred, we are
left with the only option of classifying them as 'anomalies' in
Kuhn's sense. While our bookstores show that the number of such
alleged cases have been accumulating over the years, they are no
threat to the dominant scientific paradigm, since the one thing con-
spicuous by its absence is any sign of a new paradigm or theory
that makes sense of these stories. Any attempts that I am aware of
are stuck at the level of unfalsifiable metaphysical dogma and
woolly speculation. H.H. Price, although sympathetic to the possibility of the paranormal, admits that:

*The theoretical side of psychical research has lagged far behind the evi-
dential side, and that, I believe, is one of the main reasons why the evidence itself is still ignored by so many highly educated people. It is
because these queer facts "make no sense" ... that they tend to make no
permanent impression on the mind.... If we could devise some theoretical
explanation, in terms of which the facts did make sense, it would be a
great gain. Such an explanation is needed for its own sake, and it is also
needed to get the evidence attended to and considered* (in Wheatley &
Edge [1976], p. 20).

So, to repeat, my response to Parfit's second condition is that
nothing worthy to be called an explanation has ever been offered in
connection with the paranormal. Like dualists in general, students
of psychical research can offer no significant body of theory concerning the nature of this 'res cogitans,' nor of what psychophysi-
cal laws might allow its interaction with a body. As Paul
Churchland says:

*There is no settled core of theory whose past successes have unified the
community behind it, whose current form has been shaped in response to*

past experimental failures, and whose experimental agenda drives the assembled discipline forward (p. 233).

So I admit that any paranormal events that might have occurred remain unexplained by science. However, it is often overlooked that they are equally mysterious from a Non-Reductionist perspective, which has the additional disadvantage of lacking even the beginning of any theoretical resources with which to construct an explanation.

CHAPTER FOUR

WHAT AM I?

INTRODUCTION

A s I mentioned at the beginning of the book, the primary question to be considered in this chapter is 'What kind of thing am I?' But isn't the answer obvious? I'm a person. I'm a human being. I'm a man. Not only that, but I'm a Scotsman and a philosopher. All these answers are unproblematically true, so what's the problem? The problem emerges when we consider a plausible thesis offered by David Wiggins [1980]. Take an identity statement '$a = b$,' where a and b are temporal stages of some material object that is a member of a natural kind. (A natural kind concept is a concept that plays an explanatory role in the natural sciences. Natural kinds are contrasted with artifact-kinds, which are man-made. So 'gold' and 'tiger' are natural kind terms, but 'chair' and 'guitar' are not.) Wiggins argues that the claim that a and b are stages of the same temporally-enduring object entails that a and b are identified under a sortal concept (i.e., a descriptive term) that affords the best answer to the question of what sort of thing the object in question is: "If a is the same as b, then it must also hold that a is the same *something* as b" (p. 47). This is what Wiggins calls thesis D, or the thesis of the Sortal Dependency of Identity:

D: $a = b$ if and only if there exists a sortal concept f such that
1. a and b belong to a kind that is the extension of f;
2. to say that x falls under f—or that x is an f—is to say what x is (in the sense Aristotle isolated);
3. a is the same f as b; or a coincides with b under f, i.e., coin-

cides with b in the manner of coincidence required for members of f (p. 48).

In other words, $a = b$ implies $a =_{f} b$.

The second condition above refers to 'substance-concepts,' a type of sortal concept that can apply in a present-tense form to a given object throughout its entire existence, and which specifies its 'form of life' and its 'principle of activity.' Wiggins distinguishes substance-concepts from 'phased sortal concepts,' which apply in a present-tense form only to specific portions of the individual's existence. So, for example, 'infant' and 'teenager' are among the phased sortals applicable to human beings.

While $a = b$ entails $a =_{f} b$, we can make this inference while being unable to specify f. We are only committed to saying that a and b are the same *something*—whatever the appropriate substance-concept is. The nature of f is a matter for empirical investigation, and 'f' will be a term within the taxonomy of an acceptable scientific theory.

LOCKE'S MAN/PERSON DISTINCTION

So my original question can be restated thus: What is the substance concept implicitly invoked in issues regarding identity for creatures like myself? John Locke [1690] was the first to realize that there was a philosophical problem here. Previously, the likes of Descartes would have regarded the matter as self-evident, on the assumption that since I am essentially a thinking being, any biologically based sortal concept would be unable to specify what I essentially am. Locke recognized the conflicts inherent in the dualistic conception of man.

Locke distinguished the issues of:

> i $a(t1)$ being the same *man* as $b(t2)$;
> ii $a(t1)$ being the same *person* as $b(t2)$.

He regarded the concept of 'person' as standing for "a thinking intelligent being that has reason and reflection and can consider itself as itself, the same thinking thing in different times and places" (II xxvii 9). Such a definition makes implicit reference to his criterion of personal identity, which consists in the possession of an uninterrupted flow of self-conscious awareness: "as far as this consciousness can be extended backwards to any past action or thought, so far reaches the identity of that person" (II xxvii 9).

However, as I mentioned, Locke regarded beings like ourselves as falling under another quite different sortal concept, namely *'man.'* While 'person' essentially concerns a subject as a bearer of a rational and reflective consciousness, 'man' is a biological classification, focusing on the subjects as living physical systems. It follows that the questions of whether *a (t1)* is the same man as *b (t2),* and of whether *a (t1)* is the same person as *b (t2)* must be distinguished, since their answers are determined by reference to different criteria, i.e., (respectively) whether there is a spatio-temporal track upon which both *a* and *b* can be located, and whether *b* has memories of *a*'s experiences at *t1* and at all other times leading to *t2*.

Locke believed that it was possible in principle for the criteria to diverge and thus yield different answers to the two questions above. As he states in one of his most famous passages, in the context of a thought-experiment in which two sets of memories were somehow exchanged between two brains, "Should the soul of a prince, carrying with it the consciousness of the prince's past life, enter and inform the body of a cobbler, he would be the same person with the prince" (II xxvii 15). Yet, Locke maintains, he would be the same *man* as the cobbler.

So why did Locke make the 'man'/'person' distinction, and attach so much importance to it? This distinction of sortals, and the criteria of identity underlying them, prefigures the current dispute between the Physical and Psychological Criteria. Contrary to appearance, and in particular to the last quotation, it would be rash to attribute to Locke the Cartesian doctrine that persons are essentially disembodied souls contingently embodied. It is safest to accept that here, as in other places, Locke's ambiguous use of key concepts such as 'soul' or 'consciousness' makes any attempts to maintain one consistent interpretation futile. Perhaps it is the prerogative of a pioneer to paint in broad brushstrokes, leaving the finer details to those who follow in their wake. Three main usages of 'consciousness' must be distinguished:

1. our normal waking state;
2. a state of reflective self-awareness; and most importantly
3. memory.

As for 'soul,' sometimes, as in the last quotation, he uses it in a Cartesian sense; elsewhere it seems vaguely synonymous with 'consciousness' in some rough amalgam of the usages I have just distinguished.

Breaking with Cartesianism, Locke denies the possibility of attaining knowledge of the soul:

it being, in respect of our notions, not much more remote from our comprehension to conceive that God can... superadd to matter a faculty of thinking... than he should superadd to it another substance with the faculty of thinking (IV iii 6),

and he goes on to explicitly deny that the soul is the essential bearer of personal identity. Due perhaps to a rational concern for his personal survival, he didn't risk provoking the wrath of the church by explicitly denying the existence of souls. He restricted his argument to the claim that the existence of souls, and their identity conditions, is irrelevant to the issue of personal identity. He then argued that even if souls do exist, it is possible that one soul could transmigrate from one body to another, for example in reincarnation. So in such a hypothetical case, the present mayor of Queensborough may now have what was once the soul of Socrates. But if he has no consciousness (i.e., no memory) of being Socrates and having his experiences, then, by Locke's criterion, he is not the same person as Socrates, soul or no soul. Here Locke moves away from the pure Cartesian equation of the soul with the res cogitans, which was the bearer of memories. Such a move was necessary in order to claim that memory was *constitutive* of personal identity. A Cartesian, on the contrary, would say that memory could only discover this identity.

Locke goes on to argue that if the same soul, in the same body, were to carry two separate and distinct alternating sets of thoughts and memories, then there would be two persons in one soul:

Could we suppose two distinct incommunicable consciousnesses acting on the same body, one constantly day by day, the other by night... I ask, whether the day and night man would not be two and distinct persons as Socrates and Plato (II xxvii 23).

Here, Locke dramatically anticipates modern discussions of Multiple Personality Disorder, and the challenge that such well-substantiated phenomena pose for our everyday beliefs regarding personhood and the unity of mind. Locke's main point appears to be that he regards the holding of memory *itself,* and not the possession of a soul, as the necessary and sufficient condition of personal identity.

If this is Locke's theory, then insuperable problems arise from this reluctance to regard the soul as the essential bearer of memory and of consciousness. The point is that *something* must be the bearer of these functions. They are not free-floating self-sufficient entities any more than was the grin on the face of Lewis Carroll's Cheshire Cat.

So I conclude that Locke's formulation of the man/person is incoherent. His error was to focus on memory and consciousness alone without reference to any means of embodiment. He thus places these functions in a limbo, untouched by any nomological factors that could determine what is or is not possible for them. So he cannot locate memory within any larger theory, so can't explain anything pertaining to it. I take up this task in Chapter 6.

As to why Locke placed such stress on the man/person distinction, I think we must return to 'consciousness' in its wider sense, i.e., as incorporating all the higher mental functions, the exercise of rationality, intentions, choice, etc. Locke thought that 'man,' as a biological category, could not possibly account for such matters nor, therefore, such crucial areas as moral responsibility and conscience. Like Descartes, he held to a mechanistic model of biological systems, and much of what then was a plausible theory has lost much of its force since the advent of computers, which can mechanize reason by manipulating symbols in terms of logical relations.

NATURAL KINDS AND NATURAL LAWS

Let us return to our primary question of 'What sort of thing am I?' I will now consider some ramifications of Wiggins' thesis of the Sortal Dependency of Identity, and consider the relationships between the candidate sortal concepts.

I regard 'human being' and 'homo sapiens' as bearing the same relation to each other as do 'gold' and 'the element with atomic number 79.' That is, 'human being' picks out a class of individuals in response to visible characteristics, but also makes implicit reference to a more precise principle of classification. 'Homo sapiens' supplies this latter classification, locating the class as a species within the framework of a scientific theory. Thus 'human being' and 'homo sapiens' are natural kind terms, classifying a particular kind of animal. As such, they correspond to Locke's concept of 'man.'

Next, we come to 'person.' Is it a natural kind term? A strong argument against this is based on the fact that it fails to meet a crucial test that natural kind terms must satisfy. Wiggins, following Kripke and Putnam's causal theory of reference, argues that:

any would-be determination of a natural kind stands or falls with the existence of law-like principles that will collect together the actual extension of the kind around an arbitrary good specimen of it; and that these law-like principles will also determine the characteristic development and typical history of members of this extension (p. 169).

Clearly, 'human being' and 'homo sapiens' pass this requirement. However it is not so obvious in the case of 'person.' Locke was roughly on the right track when he said that our usage of 'person' is essentially connected to the attribution of consciousness, in the wide sense of the term.

Starting from this insight, Wiggins develops what he calls the *'animal attribute'* model of personhood. He analyzes 'person' firstly in terms of a natural kind component, naming the animal species that a given individual is a member of, and secondly a *'functional'* or *'systemic'* component, involving the attribution of higher cognitive faculties. So Wiggins' schema takes the following form:

x is a person if x is an animal falling under the extension of the kind whose typical members perceive, feel, remember...; conceive of themselves as preceiving, feeling, remembering...; conceive of themselves as having a past accessible in experience-memory and a future accessible in intention, etc. (p. 171).

The dots here represent the class of intensional predicates.

Care must be taken regarding Wiggins' 'functional' component, since this term is used in a different way regarding artifact-kinds. A person is not *for* anything—i.e., a person is not 'for reasoning' in the sense that a knife is 'for cutting,' since knives were specifically designed in order to be capable of cutting. Human persons, like all animal species, are in themselves functionless. However their parts, i.e., their organs, can be regarded as having functions within the overall 'division of labor' involved in the process of life-maintenance. It is in *this* sense that the mental attributes constitutive of personhood can be regarded as functions—functions not of *persons,* but of *minds,* and hence of *brains.*

So Wiggins claims that 'person' is not a natural kind term, but a term applying to individuals falling under a subset of animal kind terms. While I am mostly in agreement over this, I would guard against any 'carbon-based chauvinism' regarding the attribution of consciousness. That is, I would leave it open, as an empirical matter, as to whether any future artifacts would satisfy an ideal Turing test and therefore warrant the ascription of personhood. Thus 'person' can be seen, rather than as applying to a subset of natural kinds, as a cross-classification that cuts across the boundaries of all kind terms, both natural and, potentially, artifactual.

I would also add that we should regard 'person' as a *secondary* classification, for two reasons. Firstly, personhood is conferred by virtue of having some physical structure capable of supporting the psychological attributes constitutive of personhood. Secondly, these psychological attributes are only possessed *contingently*. We can all sustain injury or suffer disease that would seriously diminish or destroy these functions, while the individual survives as a human being (or as whatever animal) by virtue of the continuation of the vegetative functions that keep the body alive.

'Person' cannot be treated as a natural kind concept since there are no lawlike principles that collect all the individuals in its extension, beyond the generalizations of psychology. This point is parallel to functionalism's argument against type/type identity between mental states and brain states. That is, what counts as a certain type of mental state is *anything* possessing the appropriate causal relations to certain stimuli and behavioral responses, and with other mental states. Since this specification can, in principle, be satisfied by various forms of physical embodiment, then mental states cannot be identified with any *one* of these realizations, and hence psychology is irreducible to neuroscience. Likewise in our present discussion, what counts as a person is *any* subject that possesses the cognitive and self-reflective abilities outlined by Wiggins.

Thus we see the similarity between 'person' and artifact-kind terms. Not only must the class of animal-kinds admitting prospective 'person-tokens' be kept open, but such a set of species that are so diverse in physical structure precludes the possibility of there being any nomological principles that could gather the relevant individuals, and these alone, in the way required of a natural kind term. In classifying an individual as an example of a given artifactual kind, we do not make any implicit reference to any nomological statements, nor to any theories comprising them, since the individuals in question cannot be collected as members of the given kind by reference to any such laws. Nor can they be collected by reference to some hypothesized inner structure underlying their outer characteristics. The materials and structures composing various individuals may be totally different to each other, and are in principle without limit, so no finite complete characterization can be given of the physical embodiments of all potential persons.

Likewise, the potential materials and design of a knife or a kettle are, although subject to practical limitations, still without limit. Persons can only be collected in the way we demand for members of artifact-kinds, i.e., under a functional description that is irreducible to any physical description.

Wiggins puts it this way: each token person will have a real essence, the essence of the species-kind he belongs to. There is no real essence as a person per se. To quote:

Every person would belong to some natural kind that determines a sound Leibnizian principle of identity through change for some one kind of person (human-person, dolphin-person)... indirectly this would be the real essence in virtue of which he was a person (p. 172).

As I have mentioned, to classify individuals under a substance-concept like 'human being' involves a commitment to their being a set of nomological principles that gather the extension of that kind. In fact, according to Putnam it is a condition of the *sense* of such predicates that such a set of natural laws hold for these individuals in such a way that they allow us to empirically discover what Wiggins calls the 'principle of activity' of that kind, i.e., its characteristic forms of development, and the limits of this development beyond which an individual ceases to be a member of that kind. Such a theoretical structure should provide us with principles of individuation for members of that kind, enabling us to identify and re-identify them, thus allowing an answer to any query over identity. It seems to follow that the sense of such sortal concepts precludes us from entertaining the possibility of cases involving human beings in situations that run contrary to the laws that contribute to the delimitation of that kind. For example, thought-experiments concerning individuals whose bodies could fuse together, or that could 'reproduce by natural division,' etc., shed no light upon issues of personal identity as applied to humans, as such creatures *could not* be human beings. I will elaborate on this important point in Chapter 5.

ONCE AN "f," ALWAYS AN "f"?

One other implication of Wiggins' theory is that any individual falling under a given substance-concept cannot change from being a member of such a kind to being a member of another kind and still remain the same individual, i.e., once an f, always an f. Wiggins regards spatio-temporal continuity as a necessary but not sufficient condition of identity through time, as any such identity must be identity as something—it must be sortal-covered. It goes without saying that such a condition is generally unproblematic in the real world. However, since a criterion of identity is intended to cover all possible situations, it is worth seeing how such a restriction would apply to some hypothetical problem cases.

Parfit [1984] considers a story involving a 'Teletransporter,' a machine facilitating interplanetary travel at the speed of light. It contains a 'Scanner' at departure point A that destroys my body while "recording the exact states of all my cells" (p. 199). This encoded information is transmitted by radio at the speed of light to a 'Replicator' at point B, which can be anywhere in the Universe, which "will then create, out of new matter, a brain and body exactly like mine" (p. 199). Once the Scanner is activated I will lose consciousness at point A, and wake at point B as if emerging from a short nap. But I wake in a new body, qualitatively identical to my original down to the finest structures. Since this process involves the replication of my neurons, my memories and character will be qualitatively identical to before.

Parfit devises a variant on this story involving a new improved Teletransporter incorporating a Scanner that can record the exact states of all my cells without destroying my body. However, it turns out that a design fault in the Scanner induces an irreversible cardiac disorder causing the inevitable death of the original person in a few days, while the replica at point B is unharmed. Parfit notes that there would be some overlap between the lifetimes of myself and my replica. So, in theory, we could talk to each other, and even see each other through two-way televisual phone systems. This fact of our coexistence means that I and my replica cannot be identified, due to the 'one:one' structure of identity. Our identification is also ruled out by the branching of our respective tracks of spatio-temporal coordinates.

Another point, which Parfit doesn't fully bring out, is that immediately following the creation of the replica (and I mean a minute fraction of a second) my replica and I will cease to be exactly similar. By the time it takes my replica to call assuring me of his safe arrival, our physical forms will have begun to diverge irreversibly. The two of us are now living in different environments and receiving different stimuli, in response to which our shared DNA will control and advise each cell regarding production of appropriate proteins. Since each protein selection will influence future protein selections (again in response to environmental stimuli), we will become increasingly dissimilar. Thus, if the design fault in the Scanner had been repaired prior to my entering it, and I had survived for many more years, then were my replica and I to be compared after a few years, then our qualitative similarity would be far from complete. This divergence would, of course, take place on the psychological level also. At most we would be like brothers—twins—and perhaps this is how we would come to regard one another.

Obviously these situations are impossible at present. However, Parfit doesn't think this invalidates their use as thought-experiments. He draws a distinction between the *'deeply impossible'*— cases that would contravene physical laws, from the merely *'technically impossible'*—cases whose impossibility is contingent on our technical limitations that can be overcome in the future, arguing that his examples are only technically impossible. Parfit doesn't say how you can tell whether a given case is deeply or just technically impossible. If something is deeply impossible, then it will also be impossible in practice, but the reverse is not the case. For example, a heart transplant was a technical impossibility for an 18th century barber-surgeon. From his perspective, such an operation may well have seemed deeply impossible. With hindsight, we know that it was only deeply impossible relative to his theoretical assumptions, which have now been dropped. The history of science is full of such misjudgments. All talk of deep impossibility can only be understood within the context of an underlying theory, and no theory is immune to error.

However, there are good reasons to be careful regarding the use of such thought-experiments. A cursory description (which is all that is possible in cases like Teletransportation) can easily fool us into thinking that we understand what is going on in such a situation. In fact we are glossing over a vastness of ignorance, as we couldn't begin to describe more than a tiny fraction of what would be involved here. These problems will be the topic of Chapter 5. But ignoring these doubts for the moment, I wish to investigate some implications of these thought-experiments. I will do so by devising three more thought-experiments, extending Parfit's line of enquiry. Let us call Parfit's original Teletransportation case *T1*, and his second, where the lifetimes overlap, *T2*.

T3: I have been seriously injured, and death is imminent. However, doctors offer me one alternative: Space scientists are attempting to colonize planet Z, in a distant galaxy. The trouble is that Z's atmosphere isn't conducive to human life, and settlers are confined to specially insulated environments. Intelligent life has been found on Z. In fact, these 'Z-persons' look just like humans, and possess the full range of mental phenomena constitutive of persons. The only difference is that they have an entirely different genetic structure. Anyway, the deal is this: A Scanner will record all my brain states, and this information will be sent to Z at the speed of light, whereupon my body will be destroyed. The information will be programmed into a brain in a body made in accordance with the genetic code of Z-persons. It will be arranged that I will look exactly as before, when I awaken, almost immediately after my departure from planet earth, in this new body.

T4 takes a similar scenario, except that it featured planet Z', where Z'-persons, sharing the same conditions of personhood as before, have a physical structure entirely different to our own, both on the visible macrolevel, and also on the genetic level. Thus, they look nothing like humans. I will awake in the form of a Z'-person, where psychotherapists will prepare me for the shock of my radically new appearance.

T5: Again I am terminally injured, and this time have no alternative open to me. Yet I am not despondent, since I believe that this life is not the end, and that my psychological continuity will survive the death of this body. I will lose consciousness and awaken in an exactly similar body. I will be reunited with my friends and family who have already 'passed over.'

In *T1* and *T2*, traditional substance dualism has been replaced by a new dualism of matter and *information* in the form of my 'blueprint' recording the exact states of all my cells. *T3* and *T4* focus on the information comprising the exact states of my brain cells, and incorporate the functionalist thesis that the same type of mental states can be realized in different physical systems. These cases also involve the survival of psychological continuity through a change in *kind*. That is, the person emerging from the Replicator is classed under a different substance concept from the person who entered the Scanner.

T5 is an adaptation of the Christian view of the afterlife, but in a form not fundamentally different from that of *T1*. God merely replaces the technology and somehow provides a means whereby people can identify each other, by somehow re-embodying them or giving them the appearance of such. This version of the afterlife involves no commitment to Cartesian Dualism. Indeed it seems to me that Christian thought is underdetermined regarding exactly what survives the death of the physical body. Cartesian Dualism is one development (now the dominant one), but one which is highly unsatisfactory because, among other reasons, it cannot account for how such disembodied souls can be identified and individuated. *T5* is merely another development that avoids these problems. Like all the '*T*-cases,' it involves the continuation of Relation R, i.e., psychological continuity by any causal means.

I will consider one final problem case, deriving from David Cronenberg's movie 'The Fly.' A scientist, Seth Brundle, devises a machine similar in principle to the Teletransporter, which records the genetic blueprint of the being inside the Scanner, and creates a qualitatively identical body out of new matter in the Replicator, this time located not on another galaxy, but across the room.

However, it all goes terribly wrong. When a drunken Brundle attempts to teleport himself across the room, he fails to notice that a fly has strayed into the Scanner with him. The computer records and combines both genetic codes since it has been programmed to deal with only one teleported entity at a time, and thus integrates both genetic blueprints into one hybrid structure. Thus, what emerges is a person whose genetic structure is neither completely human nor fly. At the beginning he looks and feels normal, but soon he gradually becomes transformed into a giant mutant insect. As these mutations develop, he christens himself 'Brundlefly.' So the question is 'is Brundle = Brundlefly?' By Wiggins' criteria we must say no, since there is no spatio-temporal continuity under one same substance-concept. Brundlefly is not a man, and the only natural kind concepts general enough to cover both Brundle and Brundlefly (e.g., 'organism') are excluded by this generality from qualifying as substance-concepts.

However, this judgment is extremely counterintuitive. Compare it to a similar example, *T3*, in which my mind-set is programmed into a newly created body that, although exactly like my original on the visible level, has an entirely different cellular structure. In this case, we would intuitively say that I survive. After all not only do I look the same, but I retain full psychological continuity. Yet here again, according to Wiggins, I and my Z-replica cannot be identified due to the lack of a common substance-concept between us.

CONDITIONS OF SURVIVAL

However, another option is open to us. Possibly Parfit's greatest contribution to the subject of personal identity was to turn the focus away from whether *x (t1)* was the same person as *y (t2)*, and to ask instead whether Relation R held between them. As we have seen from Chapter 2, a major reason for this shift was the existence of certain problem cases in which the question of identity was undecideable or indeterminate. Parfit argued that all that really matters in survival is captured by Relation R, i.e., the existence of certain psychological states causally connected to one's own present states.

Unlike identity, which holds between an object and itself, and is therefore not transferable, Relation R can hold between two different beings. Also unlike identity, which is an 'all or nothing' relation, Relation R can hold to different degrees.

Andrew Brennan has substantially developed Parfit's theory, replacing Relation R with the *'survival relation'* (which I will call the *'S-relation'*). Like Relation R, the S-relation can occur between two different individuals, and can hold to different degrees. However, unlike Relation R, its application is not restricted to the psychological domain, but is used by Brennan to construct a general theory of what is involved in one thing surviving in or as another thing, or in some future stage of the same continuing object. He regards this S-relation as being a more primitive relation than identity-through-time, and as being capable of explicating what matters regarding the future in cases of purported identity.

He describes the S-relation in terms of a set of 'S-conditions.' He first gives two conditions that necessarily hold when x survives in or as y:

Structure Condition: x and y must share the same structure, i.e., their component parts must be of the same relative size, shape, and positions to each other.

Causal Condition: x must play a significant and direct role in the production of y; specifically, x must be the 'prototype' of y.

A set of sufficient conditions under which x survives in y is obtained if we add a third condition:

Matter Condition: (Note that x's survival *as* y involves the holding of the S-relation to a higher degree than in x's survival *in y*.)

x survives as y if, alongside the satisfaction of the Structure and Matter Conditions, x is constructed of matter of the same kind as y.

Note that this third condition cannot be a necessary condition of the holding of the S-relation, which allows x to survive in something composed of different matter.

Before I discuss whether I survive in or as my replica in cases *T1-5*, I must note another distinction, namely that between *'types'* and *'tokens.'* It is tempting to say that an item and its replica are each tokens of the same type, with 'type' not referring to a broad class of things falling under the same sortal concept, but in the narrower sense that any replica of me would be a token of the type 'Jim Baillie.' But the situation is more complicated than this. For a fuller account we need to look at Brennan's S-conditions. Brennan says that *x* and *y* are tokens of the same type if one survives to a suitably high degree as the other. To make his point clearer, let us return to the Causal Condition, and employ yet another important distinction, between *'copying processes'* and *'production processes.'* In a copying process one item is used as a prototype, the model on which the others are based. By contrast, an example of a production process would be a machine producing soup cans, each one qualitatively identical to the next but where, taking any two consecutive products, can *n* and can *n+1*, can *n* doesn't survive as can *n+1*, since can *n* plays no causal role in the production of can *n+1*. Rather, they are both produced by the same causal processes deriving from the machine.

For Brennan, regarding copying processes, to say that two items are tokens of the same type is to say that one survives to a high degree as the other. Whereas for production processes, it is to say that they have the same sort of structure and matter, and are produced by a common causal process, without themselves being causally related. In such a case, we have replication without survival. Such an account might fit Robinson's counter-example to Parfit's Physical Spectrum (see Chapter 2), where my twin and I are not causally related, but have been produced by the same production processes, from our parents.

TELETRANSPORTATION REVISITED

I will now re-examine cases *T1—T5* in the light of this S-relation.

In *T1* (and *T5)* I clearly survive in my replica, as teletransportation is a copying process, since I am the prototype for my replica.

This analysis also applied to *T2*. It is irrelevant that I also survive in my original body for a time following the creation of my replica, as this just enables there to be survival twice over—i.e., I survive both in my original body and in my replica.

T3 is more complex in that it forces us to investigate the issue of structure in greater detail. If we say that I survive in my Z-replica, are we saying, as Brennan suggests, that the Structure Condition is more important than the Matter Condition? Or can we make the point in another way by saying that Structure at a certain level— the macro-level—is more important to the S-relation than is structure at the cellular level? The structure/matter distinction is not clear-cut since matter is intrinsically structured.

T3 has similarities with pseudomorphism, a natural phenomenon discussed by Brennan, where the atomic ingredients of a crystal are gradually replaced by different elements which, although they form unit cells of a different structure (a unit cell is the basic structure of a crystal—crystals develop through repetition of unit cells), the overall crystal shape is very similar to the way it was before these changes took place, despite these changes in the constituent matter—for example, although the atomic ingredients of fluorite (calcium and fluorine) have been replaced over time by the ingredients of quartz (oxygen and silicon).

On the other hand, in *T3* we could focus on the fact that my psychological continuity remains, despite my having been teletransported into a body with a different genetic structure. In other words, we could say that what matters is the holding of Relation R. However if we say this here and say that the physical embodiment of these psychological characteristics is of (at most) secondary importance, then we must say the same for *T4*.

Another way of developing this Parfitian position, and bringing it closer to Brennan, is to return to the Structure Condition and note that on the psychological level there exists not just a bundle of perceptions, but an essentially *structured* set of mental states and capacities. The mind functions holistically, comprising a highly complex set of mechanisms for the input, processing, storage, and retrieval of information. So in place of psychological continuity, we can talk of the survival of this cognitive structure. In normal cases, the survival of this structure rests on the survival of one's own functioning brain. Teletransportation frees us (in theory) from this requirement.

But can *T3* and *T4* be accurately described as cases of copying? It seems strange to say that something composed of an entirely different type of matter can be a copy. But let us remind ourselves that copying, like the S-relation, can hold to different degrees, and guaging to what degree a *Z*- or *Z'*-replica is a copy of me will depend on how we list our priorities. For example, we might say that my *T1* replica is a better copy than my *T3* replica (and that therefore I survive to a greater degree in my *T1* replica) because we attach value to the retention of genetic structure as well as psychological structure. Likewise, we might say that my *T3* replica is a better copy than my *T4* copy due to the retention of my original appearance. While perhaps not as important as the retention of my genetic structure, this still has great value to us, as is ironically shown by the fact that I can easily construct an example in which I survive in a body that I'd much prefer to my original body. The most important message, however, seems to be that the survival of one's psychological structure is of utmost importance to us, and this corresponds to Parfit's claims regarding Relation R.

We can apply this S-relation model to the Brundle-Brundlefly case. It is clear that the former survives in the latter to *some* degree, given the Causal Condition. There is a continuous causally related chain of events governing the relations between each contiguous pair of time-slices throughout the process of mutation. It is, in fact, a botched attempt at a copying process, with Brundle being the intended prototype. Even given the disastrous consequences, he still played a major role in the creation of Brundlefly. There is also a high degree of structural and material similarity between Brundle and Brundlefly as he was immediately following teletransportation. Even though the seeds of his imminent mutation were beginning to develop on the cellular level, his general appearance was still exactly that of Brundle. This urges the ascription of the S-relation as holding to a high degree, a claim that is strengthened when we recall that psychological continuity was completely preserved during the teletransportation. His memories remain intact, and while his character goes through a drastic set of changes (e.g., his dietary preferences) the relation of psychological continuity is flexible enough to cope with these changes. In the course of time, the wretched Brundlefly endures a succession of sudden and massive physical changes, but these do not preclude the ascription of the S-relation, or even in some cases the ascription of identity through time—we need only recall the way in which a caterpiller is transformed into a butterfly. The important factor in both cases is that the changes are not random, but are causally induced.

I feel that these arguments by Parfit and Brennan are sufficient to tell us all that matters regarding future survival. Once this content is subtracted, the further issue of identity is seen to be empty. Furthermore, since the S-relation, unlike identity, need not be sortal-governed, we can solve the problem cases that Wiggins' theory runs up against.

IS IDENTITY SORTAL-RELATIVE?

T3 opens the door to another difficult issue, concerning the dispute regarding whether identity is relative or absolute. Those holding the thesis of the relativity of identity say that the following situation is possible:

$$[(a =_f b) \ \& \ (a \neq_g b) \ \& \ (f(a) \ \& \ f(b)) \ \& \ (g(a) \ \& \ f(b))],$$

which absolutists like Wiggins deny. This is precisely the sort of situation envisaged by Locke's example of the prince and the cobbler. If we take a and b to refer to what I will call, in order not to beg any questions, the cobbler-body-being at times pre- and post-transmigration respectively, and f to refer to the sortal concept 'man,' and g to refer to 'person,' then Locke's argument amounts to the claim that a is the same *man* as b, but not the same *person* as b. I've already shown that Locke's argument is incoherent, given his treatment of memory. However, suppose it were to be updated and presented as a mind-swap, wherein the prince and the cobbler had been seized by our old friend the mad neurosurgeon, who records their respective brain-states while erasing them from the original brains, and then switches them so that the cobbler-body-being now has the memories, character traits, etc. of the prince. Here we are clearly inclined to say that the cobbler-body-being at pre-transfer time $t1$ is the same *person* as the prince-body-being at post-transfer time $t2$, yet deny that identity as a man holds between these two, as this relation holds between the $t1$ and $t2$ stages of the cobbler-body-being, and also between the $t1$ and $t2$ stages of the prince-body-being.

Let us return to *T3*. Referring to myself as *JB*, and to my Z-replica as *ZJB*, then given the complete psychological continuity between us, we are inclined to say that *JB* is the same person as *ZJB*, but not the same man nor the same animal as *ZJB*, since we are of different species. So *T3* corresponds to $[(a \neq_f b) \ \& \ (a =_g b) \ \&$ $(f(a) \ \& \ -f(b) \ \& \ (g(a) \ \& \ (g(b))]$.

So there is a slight tension in my overall position. On the one hand, I say that the most basic answer to the question 'What am I?' i.e., what is my substance concept?, is *human being*. On the other hand what seems to matter most of all is the continuation of Relation R, beyond the survival of this body, even beyond my survival as a member of this species. In other words what matters is that I survive as a *person*, or at least that some person survives who is R-related to me. Perhaps some tension is inevitable when we apply our concepts in situations so far removed from their normal uses. The important point is that my position is internally consistent. Since 'person' is not a substance-concept, 'person' is not in opposition to 'human being' regarding this question of what I am. They are not mutually exclusive categories.

APPENDIX: DISCONTINUOUS PERSONS?

Finally I will examine Wiggins' claim that for all natural kind members, '$a =_f b$' implies that a and b be located on an *unbroken* spatio-temporal track. This condition is not thought to apply to artifact-kinds. Thus if my watch is dismantled for repair, and lies in this scattered state for some time (a day or a year, it makes no difference) and is later reassembled, we would regard it as 'the same watch.' In the absence of any nomological factors pertaining to these artifactual kinds per se, and of any 'real essence' in the form of inner structure, we have nothing to go on beyond linguistic convention. It is just a fact that we *do* regard it as the same watch, and it is hard to see any utility in an alternative convention that would regard disassembly as breaching its identity conditions.

I argue that there are possible cases in which we would say that identity was retained despite the disassembly of a 'natural object,' such as a human being. Consider the rate of development of surgical techniques in recent years. Surely we agree that if a worm was cut in half then stitched back together using microsurgery, then it is the same worm as before. With humans, if one's arm is severed and stitched back on, issues of identity do not arise. But what about the brain? It is intuitively appealing to say that, in Nagel's words, 'I go where my brain goes.' But consider a case where I need brain surgery that involves the removal of my cerebral cortex, and its bisection by cutting the corpus callosum, in order to treat it and various sub-cortical structures, while my body is placed on a life-support machine. After the necessary treatments are completed, my cortex is microsurgically reunited and reattached to the rest of my brain. While leaving for the moment the question of where I was *during* the operation, we are certainly drawn to say that the survivor of the operation is still me. If one protests that the 'one:one' structure of the identity relation has been violated by the division of the cortex, then all the more reason to replace identity with the S-relation.

CHAPTER FIVE

METHODOLOGY MATTERS

USES OF THOUGHT-EXPERIMENT

This short chapter is strategically placed near the middle of the book, and represents a watershed separating two methods of enquiry that could loosely (too loosely, in fact) be respectively described as primarily 'conceptual' and 'empirical.' I now want to cast doubt on the whole foundation of the enquiries, and therefore of the conclusions, of previous chapters, and suggest a more fruitful way to investigate issues regarding personal identity. This will involve a rejection of the methodology favored by most major writers, and it will therefore result in quite a different conception of what the important issues really are.

So far I have followed a conventional approach, relying heavily on the use of thought-experiments, in accordance with a tradition that goes back to Locke. One might say that nothing has really changed in all that time—after all, what are Williams, Parfit & Co.'s neuroscientifically induced 'mind-swaps' if not Locke's prince and cobbler 'soul-swap' clad in pseudo-scientific trappings? Surveying the copious literature, it seems that one can, with sufficient ingenuity, devise some thought-experiment that purports to provide support for any criterion of personal identity, while in the near-certainty that an equally convincing counterexample lies round the corner. After a while one begins to wonder whether any progress has actually been made, and whether such techniques are appropriate to the tasks.

The most noticeable trend in much recent work has been the sheer proliferation of thought-experiments, with this expansion being not only in quantity but in diversity and ingenuity of theme, stretching our powers of credulity to the breaking point and beyond. Yet such outlandish fictions are still taken as having some bearing on life as it really is. Most philosophers have not argued for this, being content to trade on the assumption that the events described in these stories are in some sense 'possible' and thus a viable criterion of personal identity must be able to accommodate them.

Some recent authors such as Parfit and Unger take the more sophisticated line that these examples have the power to sharply expose our most deeply rooted beliefs regarding personhood and identity. They argue that since these beliefs underlie actual events in the real world, the employment of these thought-experiments is justified. As well as this capacity for the elucidation of concepts, such a method is seen as providing opportunities for conceptual revision. As Wilkes [1988] describes it, the idea is that by:

stretching a concept into the unknown one may find out more precisely what it is to which we are committed... if the concept fractures under the strain—if, that is, we would not know what to say in the hypothesized circumstances—then too the scope and limitations of the term's range and extent becomes clearer (p. 5).

To assess these claims adequately, we need to examine the application of thought-experiments in more detail. In what follows, I will draw upon recent work by Kathleen Wilkes [1988] that, if correct, has the consequence that a great deal of influential work on personal identity is fundamentally misguided. After describing and assessing her arguments I will return to some previously-discussed thought-experiments, and reevaluate them from Wilkes' perspective.

The use and justification of thought-experiments can be stated quite simply. Suppose that we want to test some theory, or to find out the consequences of some theory being true; or suppose that we want to investigate the range of application of a given concept. We can do this by asking a 'what if...?' question. In other words, we imagine that a certain state of affairs has occurred, and then try to work out the implications of such an event, and reassess the theory, concept, or whatever in the light of these judgments. Or, using 'possible worlds' terminology, we can say that such events have happened in some possible world, and then try to work out what else follows regarding this world. However, it is essential that these events take place in "a world like our own in all relevant aspects, except for the existence in that world of the examined phenomena" (p. 2). In other words, "The possible world is our world, the world described by our sciences, except for one distinguishing difference. So we can know or assume everything else that it is relevant to know, in order to assess the thought-experiment" (p. 8).

It is not the case that 'anything goes' in the employment of thought-experiments. They are quite literally experiments, and as such are bound by the same methodological canons as all experiments that aim to tell us about the world. One major constraint is that one must be able to state the background conditions against which the event under scrutiny takes place. This is essential because the thought-experiment is specifically designed to draw out the consequences of an event, which can only be done if we can ensure that these consequences could not be due, in sum or in part, to other auxiliary factors. So, since we require that the possible world in which the event takes place be like *our* world with the exception of this one alteration under scrutiny, we must ensure that the background to this event is well-specified, and is consistent with conditions in our world.

When such requirements are fulfilled, then the derivation of the consequences of the experiment is a relatively straightforward matter. Such successful thought-experiments occur mainly in the natural sciences. By contrast, the use of thought-experiments in the philosophical study of personal identity has been, according to Wilkes, one long catalogue of disaster. In cases from the sciences, we not only see the satisfaction of this demand for strictly defined experimental conditions (in particular when the experiment takes place within a closed system), allowing a complete description of the relevant background, but we also have the advantage of an explicit and developed *theory* governing the experiment, couched in strictly defined theoretical terms, allowing any assumptions and entailments to be correspondingly clear-cut. It it thus a straightforward matter to determine whether or not a particular factor is relevant to the results achieved.

ABUSES OF THOUGHT-EXPERIMENT

By contrast, the 'folk-psychological' concepts in which theories of personal identity are couched are not capable of such strict definitions, and thus any inferences we make are not straightforward, but are problematic and without a firm basis. We are left at the level of deciding 'what we would say if...' with no trustworthy means of evaluating such conclusions over and above our intuitions which, of course, are conditioned by our other beliefs. Thus:

when we are dealing with the rich and riotous chaos of commonsense concepts, we are dealing with terms that generally do not pick out natural kinds, and so there is no body of explicit theory or shared and agreed generalisations about them; we are rather dealing with implicit and partial, rough and ready assumptions. Hence the importance of intuition grows in direct proportion to its precariousness" (Wilkes p. 16).

However, the main problem for typical philosophical thought-experiments has not been due to the vagueness of natural language, but through failing to fix background conditions to the experiment sufficiently. In the absence of these specifications, the experiment fails to be adequately described, and thus we cannot tell if the hypothetical situation depicted therein is a real possibility.

We are now getting to the heart of the matter. Philosophers have often made an illicit jump from the fact that they can, in a sense, 'imagine' or 'conceive of' some state of affairs, to the claim that such a situation is a real possibility. Thus Descartes reckoned that he could imagine his continuing to exist as a disembodied thinking being, and took this feat of suspended disbelief as proving that such a situation could actually occur. In fact, rather than to describe his error as being in some unjustified jump from 'imaginability' to 'possibility,' it is more accurate to say that whatever the mental imagery involved in such a thought-experiment, one *cannot* imagine being disembodied. It only *seems* as if you can imagine this, due to the cursory description given to the content of the experiment. Once you try to think it through, things look less obvious. As I argued against Swinburne, what would such an existence be like? How could you move without muscles or a motor cortex? How could you perceive without sense organs? As Wilkes says in her general point about such cases:

the fact that we may not have identified all the relevant laws makes no difference, except to mislead; since we are largely ignorant of these and their interconnections, it of course seems easy to imagine the transformations; the obtrusive facts are not there to obtrude (p. 31).

Likewise, it is easy to be fooled into thinking that you can imagine a bar of iron floating in a pool of water. But once the physical properties of both substances are considered, and once the background conditions are specified to rule out invisible strings suspending the bar, unusual anti-gravitational forces, etc., it soon becomes clear that no matter what mental images you are having, they are not about iron and water.

It is not enough to say that the event described in the thought-experiment be logically possible. Rather, it must be *'theoretically possible,'* i.e., there must be a satisfactory description of its background conditions that provides us with a *theory* of the kinds of objects involved, enabling us to decide whether the hypothetical event is a real possibility. Wilkes describes this notion of theoretical possibility as providing:

something between stringent essentialism and loose conventionalism, something that will allow us to insist... that the human species is a kind governed by law, while not denying that some of these laws may fail to hold of individual members of the species (p. 28).

I will pursue this theme by developing Wiggins' ideas (as discussed in Chapter 4) together with the semantic theory of Hilary Putnam [1970].

We can follow Putnam in saying that natural kind terms are *'law cluster concepts,'* where there is a determinate set of *'core facts,'* most of which must hold in order for a given object to qualify as a member of the kind in question. This cluster of laws will limit what is theoretically possible for a member of that kind, and help determine which presuppositions and implications are relevant to any thought-experiment involving a typical member of that kind. Wilkes points out that laws governing biological kinds do not apply in isolation, totally independent of one another, but on the contrary are closely interrelated. So:

it will be rare that we find an isolated breach of a single law. It is far more likely that such a violation will have consequential effects upon other laws, where such laws are either at the same sort of level (in the same or a different theory) or where they are more fundamental laws that describe the operations and the limitations of such higher-level laws as the law we are supposing to be violated, [thus] ...the physical, as well as the mental, is holistic, with laws arranged in a systematic hierarchy of mutual dependence (p. 30).

Wilkes' arguments have yet to find much favor. However, one recent author who at least acknowledges the importance of questions regarding methodology is Peter Unger [1990]. He accepts that if the description of an example is vague and sparse, then it is unlikely to provide reliable insight into our beliefs and attitudes regarding identity. Likewise, if an example clashes with our deeply held beliefs regarding what is possible, this is prima facie reason to reject the example, or give little weight to its conclusions. Thus he argues that:

The descriptions of our examples should be in at least rough conformity with the main outlines of our worldview: This is not conformity with some basic scientific principles, which may be known only to some few scientists; but, rather, it is conformity with propositions that are central to our common fabric of belief. When an example asks you to suppose a central belief of yours to be false, or otherwise to be abandoned, various of your other beliefs will be dragged in its wake. Then, relative to the context of the exercise, you might not be left with a firm basis of belief from which to respond to the example. In that situation, your attendant responses, inso-

far as they are available at all, are liable to be rather weak, conflicting
and indecisive.... The descriptions of our examples should be reasonably
rich in those details that are relevant to asking questions that we pose
about the cases: Without these helpful indications, we may again be left up
in the air, with no firm attitudinal basis for responding (p. 8–9).

Now all this strikes me as being good sense, and as being in full
accord with Wilkes. However, Unger sharply contrasts with Wilkes
over how these methodological principles are applied, since
Unger's book contains numerous ingenious variations of the usual
thought-experiments that Wilkes condemns. How he renders these
compatible with our normal worldview I do not know. However, I
suspect that there is a fair degree of subjectivity regarding where
one draws the line over the legitimacy of thought-experiments. For
example, I am particularly partial to Nozick's 'experience machine'
example which, despite the claims of the burgeoning 'virtual reality' industry, is still far from being a reality at present.

With all this in mind, let us examine a typically adventurous
thought-experiment (from Parfit [1971]) wherein we are asked to
consider what we would say if people could divide like amoebae.
So, if A split to form B and C, how can A be the same person as
both B and C? As neither B nor C? As B but not as C? As C but not
as B? I needn't repeat all the problems with each choice.

It should now be fairly clear that we cannot leave this state of
affairs at this level of description, as this would involve superim-
posing this radically different form of human development over our
world with its cluster of laws governing biological development,
and then assuming that everything goes on otherwise as normal.
Firstly, the background conditions have not begun to be described,
and since such a development is taken to occur outside the strictly
defined limits of a scientific experiment, these background conditions will need to include a significant proportion of the possible
world. Indeed it is hard to specify the limit on the amount of information required in order to derive reliable conclusions from this
example. When we attempt to spell out all that is required, the
whole enterprise descends into farce. I can do no better than to
quote once again from Wilkes:

It is obviously and essentially relevant to the purposes of this thought-experiment to know such things as: How often? Is it predictable? Or sometimes predictable and sometimes not, like dying? Can it be induced, or prevented? Just as obviously, the background society, against which we set the phenomenon, is now mysterious. Does it have such institutions as marriage? How would that work? Or universities? It would be difficult, to say the least, if universities doubled in size every few days, or weeks, or years. Are pregnant women debarred from splitting? The entire background here is incomprehensible. When we ask what we would say if this happened, who, now, are we? (p. 11).

We can now relate all of this to the point about the cluster of laws that limits the real possibilities for members of natural kinds. It is clear that any possible world in which persons could split like amoebae would be highly different from our world in ways we can hardly imagine. Thus we don't know to what extent, and in what ways, the background conditions to this example are consistent with the real world. Also, any beings that could divide like this would require a physical structure radically unlike our own. Thus they could not be the same species as us, and may be individuated along entirely different principles to us. So no matter what our conclusions are about the identity-conditions for these creatures, we cannot use them to derive conclusions about ourselves. But this, of course, was the whole point of devising the example in the first place.

HUMAN FREEDOM AND NATURAL LAWS

It might be argued that all this talk of law clusters constraining human possibilities views humans as passive slaves of immutable laws that strictly and absolutely delimit their range of possible activities and developments, and that such a depiction ignores the fact that human beings are active participants in a dynamic, changing universe. It is becoming clear that human knowledge and expertise (and abuses thereof) have reached a level where we ourselves now constitute an active initiatory factor in determining the development of our species, and that of other species. Take genetic engineering, for example. Or consider the consequences of the destruction of the tropical rain forest, including the greenhouse effect that could possibly involve large climatic disruption. While I don't imagine that we will start splitting or fusing, or anything as outré as that, who can predict into what forms our species will evolve in order to survive in the face of such challenges? And who is to say, by some principle, that such future beings would not be human?

While our physical structures place us under significant practical limitations at any given time, they do not do so completely. In other words, any Wiggins-style 'principle of activity' is not static and determinate, but is open-ended, with ourselves playing a part in its development. To talk in Sartrean terms for the moment, our principle of activity is waiting to be actualized by us, and has no 'essence' prior to this.

I make these rather melodramatic remarks as a prelude to discussing one prominent example that is far from the excesses of amoeba-like fission, fusion, time-travel, and suchlike, and focuses on a more credible case that involves the possible application of human ingenuity in initiating certain events that would seem to force us into making radical revisions to our beliefs about personal identity and unity. It is of course an empirical matter, but it seems to me that one type of 'splitting' is a real possibility for the near future, namely the transplantation of neural structures. There has been an extraordinary rate of development in the practice of transplant surgery, in the techniques of microsurgery, in overcoming problems of rejection, etc., all within my lifetime. For example, thirty years ago a successful heart transplant was considered an impossible dream. The dream was realized in the '60s, and techniques have since been refined to the extent that a person can now survive the transplant of heart, lungs, and liver. Add this to the fact that numerous experiments have been performed in which various parts of the brains of salamanders have been exchanged. Also, as Wilkes informs us, entire heads of monkeys have been swapped (although the resulting creatures only have a zombie-type existence, since so many nerve connections cannot be repaired). Given such achievements, which until recently would have been judged to have been 'deeply impossible,' we should be cautious about making the same mistake regarding human brain transplants or hemisphere transplants.

Now do these considerations go against Wilkes' critique of the use of thought-experiments in philosophy? I do not think so. We can render compatible the two divergent strands by saying the following:

1. What is and what is not theoretically possible is a function of a given background theoretical structure. There is no 'theoretical possibility' as seen from an outside, theory-free standpoint.

2. No theory, no matter how well-corroborated, is immune from error, even fundamental and widespread error.

3. So, if some state of affairs S is judged, on the basis of theory 1, to be theoretically impossible, and theory 1 is replaced in time by theory 2, it does not follow that S is theoretically impossible by theory 2. We have no unified and complete theory of human beings that could lay down precise limits regarding possible states of affairs for humans for all future times. We have a variety of theories in physics, chemistry, biology, psychology, sociology, etc., all at various degrees of maturity.

Taking all three points together, we don't know if philosophical thought-experiments depict real possibilities. Some well may. However, it does not follow that such examples yield trustworthy conclusions about the real world, since we lack the ability to fill out the background adequately. It is one thing to say that we don't know that the situation depicted therein is impossible. It is another thing entirely to say that it is a real possibility, and, as Wilkes says, "ignorance is a poor justification for any experiment, scientific or philosophical" (p. 20). So we have no real grounds for saying that such situations are real possibilities. On the contrary, the fact that we tend to be unable to flesh out the background is evidence against their possibility, despite the limitations of any theory we currently employ.

THOUGHT-EXPERIMENTS REASSESSED

I will now return to the main philosophical thought-experiments on personal identity, and reassess their worth in accordance with the conclusions of this chapter. One useful distinction that can be made is between those involving 'brain-transfer' and those involving 'mind-transfer.' In other words, the first sort involve the removal and subsequent replacement of neural structures, whereas the second concentrate on the mental contents themselves.

As I have mentioned, philosophers are often far too lax in their talk of brains, equating the brain per se with the cerebral cortex. Now if we are literally talking about a *brain* transplant, then it is not enough to remove the cortex. The brain stem will need to be removed. And what of the spinal cord? This is integrally connected with processes required for the possibility of conscious experience. Can *it* be removed? The central nervous system functions as one integrated system, and any distinction between parts that can be called 'brain,' and those that cannot, will be rather grey. As well as this conceptual issue, we don't know what would happen if all these structures were exchanged and placed in new bodies. We are not monkeys, and any results regarding the swapping of monkey heads is not conclusive evidence that a brain-swap or a head-swap is a real possibility for human beings. And even if it succeeded on the basic physical level, and both humans survived the operation, we don't know what state their higher cognitive faculties would be in. Granted, we have a strong hunch that a person will wake up in the body into which his brain was transplanted, but such guesswork is not a strong enough foundation on which to base a philosophical theory.

I have two points to make on the subject of cortical or hemispherical exchange (e.g., 'My Division') Firstly, as I argue in Chapter 7, one of the premises in such thought-experiments is wrong. A split-brain patient—whose corpus callosum has been sectioned—does *not* have 'two minds' and is *not* 'two persons.' Furthermore, the *brain* is not split, but rather the means for direct intercommissural information exchange is removed. But any frag-

mentation or division in consciousness that results from this operation takes place against a background of great unity, both structural
and functional, via the intact subcortical structures. Secondly, we
have the problem of ignorance again. We do not know what would
happen if one cerebral hemisphere was transplanted into a cortexless skull. We do not know if the memories, character traits, etc. of
the hemisphere's original 'owner' would be preserved intact, or if
the other person's subcortical brain systems would dominate, or
whether they would integrate, conflict, or, more likely, whether
death would ensue.

Thirdly, let us examine thought-experiments involving brain
exchange on a cell-by-cell scale, such as in Parfit's Physical
Spectrum. Such stories seem to be based on at least one false
premise concerning the nature of memory storage in the brain. It is
assumed that memories come in discrete quanta, one (or however
many) located *within* each neuron. So the neuron itself is assumed
to be the container of memories. But strong experimental evidence
suggests that long-term memories are stored in the form of an
altered electrical resistance in the synapses *between* neurons. So
we cannot 'atomize' the brain to achieve any 'neuron:memory'
correspondence, as there is an irreducibly *relational* factor between
neurons regarding memory.

Regarding experiments where a qualitatively identical brain or
body is created from the original prototype, I have little more to
say than to repeat our virtually complete ignorance over what
would be involved in this, so we have no way of telling whether it
is theoretically possible.

I will now consider 'mind-swaps,' and offer my solution to
Williams' puzzle from "The Self and the Future," which has been
hanging since Chapter 2. Examining Williams' two cases in the
light of the considerations of this chapter, it is obvious that we can
hardly begin to describe the conditions under which these 'mind-
swaps' could be performed, and thus we are not justified in taking
them to be real possibilities. We can hardly conceive of the technology that would be involved. How could someone's entire
'mind-set'—memories, beliefs, character traits, etc.—be extracted

from a brain, and then be recorded and stored in some structurally isomorphic form in a machine? How could this information be then 'programmed' into another brain? How could these mental contents be entirely erased without causing brain damage or death? Could one withstand the shock of such an operation, either physically or psychologically? Would the 'new mind' have to cope with problems of rejection of the kind that must be overcome in organ transplants? Case 1 assumes that the personality is unaffected by being placed in a new body. What could possibly justify this assumption? I could go on, but I think that the point has been made.

My guess is that Williams, like so many, has been seduced by the widespread use of the computer analogy with the mind, and has fallen into the trap of implicitly employing a strict hardware/software distinction, so that one software system (i.e., a mind) can be removed from one hardware system (i.e., a body) and be placed in another, yet be intrinsically unchanged.

The illusion of coherence in Williams' examples is purely due to our ignorance of many of the 'obtrusive facts' that might get in the way. So we can now see the roots of Williams' puzzle. *Both* the contrary conclusions that we are led to by the respective cases are unwarranted and untrustworthy, as they are based on slightly different but equally inadequate descriptions of the conditions involved in such experiments. Our intuitions are conditioned by our beliefs, and we are not in a position to acquire a set of well-justified beliefs regarding the outcomes of this pair of thought-experiments. The fact that the two cases that elicited the contrary responses were virtually alternative descriptions of the same state of affairs merely exposes how 'out of their depth' our intuitions are when confronted with such cases.

WHAT MATTERS IN SURVIVAL?

With all this in place, we can now return to the Reductionist thesis 7 (see page 8), namely Parfit's claim for the priority of Relation R over personal identity. As we have seen, Parfit has argued that what matters is not essentially whether *I* survive at some future time, but whether *someone* will exist who is related to me by Relation R, i.e., psychological continuity by any means. In other words, it doesn't matter whether this person is *me,* as long as he or she is causally related to me in such a way that psychological continuity—particularly memory—is preserved.

Recall his use of 'Teletransportation' examples to charm our intuitions past their immediate resistance. Suppose that this hypothetical machine were to destroy my body, while recording the exact states of all my cells so that it has a complete physical description of me. It then uses this information to create another body that is exactly similar to my original, both physically and psychologically. He will look exactly like me, will share my old beliefs and desires, and will have all the same experiential memories of my life. In other words, this person would be an exact duplicate of me.

Parfit argues that nothing that really matters would be lost in such a situation. Whether or not *I* survive, the preservation of my psychological continuity is *just as good* as its preservation through my survival in my original body. In other words, what really matters regarding survival is Relation R, not personal identity.

The plausibility of Parfit's examples is enhanced by their being presented in first person singular terms. I am invited to imagine all this happening to *me,* and am encouraged to accept that since the person emerging from the Replicator looks exactly like me, and, in particular, since the subjective aspect, the 'what it's like to be me' seems unchanged, then what else could possibly matter? However, things look rather different when we examine Parfit's theory from a third personal perspective. Parfit is committed to taking the same attitude to other people—that is, that it doesn't matter if they survive, as long as some persons survive that are psychologically continuous with them. It would follow from this thesis that the replacement of those I care about by duplicates should be considered as no real loss at all. For example, should my wife be 'teleported' so that her body is destroyed and she is replaced by a duplicate, then I would have no good reason not to transfer totally my love for her onto this replica.

This view is opposed by Peter Unger [1990], for whom such a

replacement would be a personal disaster. He imagines being forced to choose between two options. In Option One, he continues to live with his wife Susan; in Option Two, she is transported to some parallel universe, while Unger remains here with a duplicate of her. He responds that:

As would many in similar circumstances, I choose Option One. Evidently, I do not just care about the very many highly specific qualities my wife has, or just about there being only one woman on earth with just these specific qualities, or just about spending much time, in exclusive arrangements, with the only woman on earth with just those specific qualities. Quite beyond any of that, I care about the one particular person who is my wife: I care about Susan and, as well, I care about the continuance of my particular relationship with her (p. 276).

So Unger is saying that we place intrinsic and irreducible value on certain individuals, and on our relationships with them, and therefore that a duplicate would not retain 'all that mattered' of the original person. So it is just false to say that we have no preferences regarding whether to continue living with one's wife or with a duplicate.

Unger devises another thought-experiment to make this point. Suppose that a duplicate of your daughter has been recently created, and you are forced to choose between two options. In Option One, (i) your daughter continues to live with you, (ii) her duplicate is killed, (iii) you are subjected to a period of torture by electric shock. In Option Two, (i) your daughter is killed, (ii) the duplicate takes her place in your life, (iii) you receive $100 million. In both cases, you will have no memory of your choice. For simplicity's sake, let us add that in Option Two your daughter will be killed in such a way that she will have no mental or physical suffering. As before, Unger contends that he, and we, would choose Option One, and that such an example shows that we attach intrinsic value to the lives of specific individuals, and to our ongoing relations with them (which requires the survival of ourselves, and not just a duplicate). Therefore, Relation R does not contain all that matters.

This disagreement between Parfit and Unger is partly due to a difference in the aims of their work. Unger explicitly affirms the conservative nature of his project, namely to identify and describe our actual beliefs and values regarding survival and identity. Parfit is a revolutionary, arguing that we need to radically reassess our attitudes to our selves and our futures. So while I concur with Unger that nothing would induce me to reject my wife in favor of some duplicate of her, it should be pointed out that Parfit accepts that most people would respond in the same way. However, he would insist that we would be being irrational in doing so. So the real issue is not about what our actual preferences would be, but whether they can be rationally justified. I will argue that any present claim regarding the rationality or irrationality of any such preference is unwarranted.

Unger is correct in his more general thesis that we often place special value on certain individual objects, so that no duplicate could adequately replace them for us. If a museum pays millions of dollars for a Van Gogh, it will matter a great deal to them whether they have acquired the real thing or merely an extremely accurate forgery. Or consider two white Fender Stratocaster guitars, in equally good condition and with no significant material differences between them. If one of these guitars was once owned by Jimi Hendrix, it thereby attains a greater value than others of its type.

However, these sorts of cases are the exception rather than the rule. Generally we have little or no personal attachments to specific objects. Consider the typewriter I'm now using, the paper I'm typing on, the chair I'm sitting on, the exquisite shirt I'm now wearing. In fact, in the case of virtually everything in my office, I would be completely indifferent when confronted with a choice between keeping them or having them replaced by duplicates. The special value conferred on a Van Gogh painting or a Hendrix guitar does not rest on any intrinsic *properties* that these objects possess, but in their *causal relationships* to persons who are held in high esteem. This accounts for the veneration of religious relics such as the Turin Shroud, and explains why the question of its 'authenticity' was such a big issue for so many people. As my next examples illustrate, some objects may attain this special status through their connection to some important event. This value is non-transferable.

When we consider nonconscious material objects, and in particular when we consider artifacts, we can have extremely trustworthy intuitions over whether or not a teletransported duplicate would retain 'all that matters' of the original. We can do this because the teletransportation examples are similar in relevant ways to real-life events. Let us consider another example. When I purchased my wedding ring, it was chosen from a row of several qualitatively identical rings. At that time, any of those rings would have been equally suitable. Thus, had the ring I selected fallen down a hole in the display cabinet so as to not be immediately retrievable, then any other of these rings would have been equally suitable.

However, once my ring had taken part in my marriage ceremony, it took on a unique value that is not transferable to any other qualitatively identical ring. In fact, I foolishly lost my ring a few days after the ceremony, and it was no consolation to know that I could go back to the jewelers for another one just like it. So, since I know that no conventionally-produced duplicate ring would do, I can make the same judgment about a duplicate produced by teletransportation. It doesn't matter how the duplicate is made—it is not the original ring, and does not have the special value attached to the original, grounded in the marriage ceremony.

On the other hand, if I lend my copy of 'Reasons and Persons' to a colleague, who then loses, it, then a replacement copy will be perfectly satisfactory. So, as before, I can confidently say that the replacement of my book by a teletransportationally produced duplicate will cause me no grief. I can predict and rationally justify my responses to these hypothetical examples because they do not require large-scale disruption to our attitudes about rings, books, etc....

One way of making this point is to say that the type/token distinction is well-integrated into our general set of attitudes to manmade objects. Given our familiarity with processes of mass production, we accept that when all things are equal (i.e., in the absence of any special value-conferring relationships), one token of a specific type is as good as any other. All that the introduction of teletransportation does is to devise a different means for producing more tokens of preexisting types. Apart from that, our set of general beliefs, preferences and values concerning these artifacts remains relatively untouched. Thus I can explain the rationality of my preference for my original wedding ring over a teletransported duplicate purely in terms of the rationality of my account of why *any* replacement ring would be inadequate in real life.

However, we cannot use these considerations to argue for or against the rationality of preferences in the case of original versus duplicate wives. Unlike in the previous examples, nothing in our experience even remotely resembles the replacement of a person by a duplicate. Each person is qualitatively unique, and so the type/token distinction plays no corresponding role in our attitudes to individual persons. Of course, we can say that each of us is a token of the type 'person,' but that is a different issue. There is no type/token distinction as applied to types such as 'Jim Baillie,' 'Derek Parfit' or 'Peter Unger.' Should teletransportation ever become a reality, and this distinction gain a foothold in our lives, then our attitudes to persons would suffer such an enormous disruption that the outcome cannot now be predicted. All that we can say with certainty is that such a fundamental change in our situation would leave our worldview totally altered.

This is why we cannot make any judgments regarding whether or not I am rational in preferring to continue living with my wife rather than with a duplicate. The rationality of a preference or belief is not an intrinsic property of that individual state considered in isolation, but is determined by its relationships to the evidence and to our other attitudes. In other words, whether my preference for my wife over any duplicate is a rational preference will depend on how well this preference coheres with my entire network of beliefs, preferences and values. However, this degree of fit cannot be ascertained at present, because the introduction of duplicate persons would cause a vast rupture to our cognitive map. Firstly, we have no way of telling which attitudinal changes would occur to accommodate this new state of affairs. Secondly, the assessment of the rationality of my preference in term of my *present* attitudes is not relevant, since many of these beliefs, preferences and values would be rendered obsolete by such developments. So I conclude, in opposition to both Parfit and Unger, that any present judgment on the rationality of preferences in such a hypothetical situation are not justified.

CHAPTER SIX

MEMORY

LOCKE'S CRITERION

I will begin this chapter with a detailed discussion of John Locke's memory-based theory of personal identity. This may appear as if I am trying to smash an egg with a sledgehammer, i.e., devoting too much time and energy in attacking a position that can be easily dismissed. However, it should be kept in mind that Locke's theory has been the starting point for virtually all contemporary forms of the Psychological Criterion, and while these latter theories involve significant modifications and improvements on Locke, I will argue that they still retain some of his errors.

Locke explicitly associates the holding of personal identity, and indeed of personhood itself, with the ability to remember one's past experiences:

"As far as this consciousness can be extended backwards to any past action or thought, so far reaches the identity of that person" (II xxvii 9); "That with which the consciousness of this present thinking thing *can* (my italics) conjoin itself, makes the same person, and is one self with it, and with nothing else, and so attributes to itself and owns all the actions of that thing as its own, as far as that consciousness reaches, and no further" (II xxvii 17).

Let us examine the second of these two passages. Antony Flew [1951] notes that this passage can be interpreted in two different ways, depending on how the term 'can' is understood. It can firstly be interpreted in the 'logical' sense, i.e., as 'can without contradiction'; or secondly in the 'factual' sense, as 'can as a matter of fact.'

Flew argued that Locke is claiming that having memories of one's past experiences constitutes the necessary and sufficient condition for the holding of personal identity. Thus, on the logical sense of 'can,' we have the claim that x $(t1)$ is the same person as y $(t2)$ if and only if x and y are both persons, and it is logically possible that y can remember what x experienced at $t1$.

However, this is far too lax to be a satisfactory criterion of personal identity, admitting too many undesirable cases. For example, there is no formal contradiction involved in a hypothetical case wherein various laws of nature are broken so that I now remember experiencing certain events as they were originally experienced by Napoleon. However, if I remember experiences that were undergone by Napoleon, then by the above criterion, I must be Napoleon. Suppose I then remember experiences from the point of view of Admiral Nelson. It follows that I am Nelson. But if so, it follows from the transitivity of the identity relation that Napoleon and Nelson are the same person. Since this conclusion is false, yet the argument is logically valid, it follows that at least one of the premises is wrong. I needn't list all the absurdities that would ensue from such an identification, e.g., one both being and not being one-armed in 1805, etc..

Turning to Flew's second interpretation of Locke, we have the claim that x $(t1)$ is the same person as y $(t2)$ if and only if x and y are both persons, and y can, as a matter of fact, remember what x experienced at $t1$. (Strictly, x and y are not persons, but person-stages.) This criterion, by contrast, is far too strict. In fact, it would exclude *all* actual cases of identity, since we all forget *some* of our experiences, and this criterion demands that all our experiences be remembered, and indeed constantly remembered at all stages of one's life. Since I will at $t2$ only remember some of my experiences at $t1$ and at other times, it follows that Locke cannot identify me at $t2$ with any *person* at all at $t1$ or at other times.

'MEMORY' DISMANTLED

An immediate response to my objections is that they merely highlight the fact that there was a virtual absence of theory in Locke's day concerning the nature of memory, beyond it being regarded as some form of 'storehouse of ideas' in the mind. (This can only be a metaphor, since Locke held the dualistic view that the mind is non-material, and therefore not extended in space. But how then could it 'store' anything?) Until recently, most theories had assumed the existence of a 'memory trace' or 'engram' physically embodying each memory. These memory traces are assumed to be representations of past experiences, each being in some way a structural analogue of its corresponding experience. But there remains great conceptual obscurity regarding exactly how such a structural isomorphism can take place. No memory trace has ever been discovered, due no doubt in part to this conceptual difficulty entailing that we don't really know what to look for. The memory trace remains a theoretical entity, inferred to exist because to deny its existence in some form would imply that memory involved 'action at a distance,' and we strongly believe that there can be no direct causation through a temporal gap. It is assumed that we require a continuous causal chain, with some form of physical basis, to bridge the gap between the times of the experience and of its later recall. This physical basis, whatever it is, has been called a memory trace. Given our ignorance of the nature of memory, we have viewed it in terms of analogies with things that we understand better, from Plato's impressions in wax, through Penfield's video recorder playbacks, to contemporary computer models in terms of input, storage and readout.

The newly emerging Connectionist model of mind does not posit any permanent memory traces, favoring a dispositional theory of memory. I shall not consider this any further, since the connectionist model is still in its infancy, and its implications for any Psychological Criterion are by no means clear.

Scientists have made various distinctions regarding different types of memory. At the very least, these categories are useful in describing and ordering diverse phenomena, and their cautious employment will enable me to take traditional philosophical theories of memory and personal identity considerably further. Let us begin by dismantling the old *unitary* concept of memory, and bring in a tripartite division of registration, storage, and retrieval. One might employ the distinction between information storage and retrieval to argue for a neo-Lockean criterion that does not demand that any stored memory must be retrievable at any given time, but merely that all experiences be stored, as memory traces, throughout one's life, whether or not they can in practice be retrieved and recalled to conscious awareness.

Locke, of course, would find such a revision incomprehensible, since he had inherited from Descartes the thesis of the 'incorrigibility of the mental,' the idea that all that one knows must be 'known to be known.' He could not accommodate the idea of information that was both stored 'in the mind,' yet beyond the reach of conscious awareness:

that consciousness which is inseparable from thinking, and, as it seems to me, essential to it, it being impossible for any one to perceive without perceiving that he does perceive... consciousness always accompanies thinking (II xxvii 11).

MEMORY STORAGE

Can a credible criterion be based on the thesis that the continuity of memory necessary to preserve identity is that the memories are stored, whether or not they are retrieved? The problem is whether there is any evidence that memories are stored, apart from their retrieval into conscious awareness. How can we tell whether the memory of a certain event is either (i) irretrievably lost, or (ii) stored, but not yet consciously recalled? Is it possible that *every* experience is stored for one's entire life, and can be retrieved if one is presented with the appropriate stimulus? The major problem with such a claim is that it is unfalsifiable, since the non-retrieval of a given memory can always be attributed to the lack of suitable stimuli, rather than its no longer being stored. Even if the theory is unfalsifiable, is there any evidence in favor of it?

Wilder Penfield's experiments, where points on the exposed temporal cortex were stimulated with live electrodes while patients remained conscious, were once thought to provide such evidence. Patients reported experiencing extremely vivid sensations on being stimulated by the electrodes, and Penfield took these experiences to be recollections of past experiences. He then theorized that every individual memory is stored in some specific and stable location in the temporal cortex; and secondly that if a given point were stimulated, whether artificially or 'naturally' in the process of brain function, then the corresponding memory would be recalled.

However, both Penfield's experimental results and his theoretical model have been discredited. He thought that when we pay conscious attention to something, we then 'record' this experience, which is stored in some structurally isomorphic form within the temporal cortex. So he saw memory in terms of a tape-recorder model, where every experience is stored completely and, given the appropriate stimulus, can be 'played back' in full. But his results are far too humble to warrant such a dramatic conclusion. Firstly it should be kept in mind that all these experiments were performed on epileptics (in fact, the phenomenon was discovered by accident while attempting to reduce seizures) and so the findings do not necessarily apply to 'normal' brains. Secondly, the phenomena were extremely rare—out of 520 patients, 40 reported having *some* sensation whenever the electrode touched the cortex; out of these, only 12 could be proposed as possible cases of genuine recall— i.e., less than 3% of his total patients. Thirdly, of this 3%, no independent check was ever made to corroborate the claim that these experiences were real memories. Fourthly, it is possible that they were genuine, but that their recall was a mere coincidence, not caused by the electrode. Fifthly, there is always the possibility (albeit an unfalsifiable one) that if another point on the cortex had been stimulated at the same time, rather than the original point, then the same experience would have been recalled. Penfield himself made an observation that would seem to go against his theory when he noted that if the same point were stimulated twice, a few minutes apart, then the same experience was not summoned again.

In studies of people who have had significant areas of their cortex removed (e.g., up to 40%), there seem to be no specific and selective gaps in memory, as would seem to be implied by a theory that posits a precise, static 'one:one' correlation between memories and points on the cortex. This would still allow the possibility that each memory has several memory traces, distributed throughout the cortex. Finally, from an evolutionary point of view, it is surely unnecessary to have a brain that stores everything, every last insignificant detail. It would make more sense to have a brain that actively selects rather than passively records, retaining the information that appears to be useful and relevant to the future.

PARFIT'S PSYCHOLOGICAL CRITERION TESTED

Returning to Locke, one of the most noteworthy attacks on his theory, and the one most responsible for the modern modifications to it, is Reid's argument that by Locke's theory, "a man may be, and at the same time not be the same person that did a particular action" (p. 114). Reid exploys the famous argument of the officer who had been flogged as a boy for stealing apples from an orchard, who had later captured a standard on his first military campaign, and who had ended his career as a general. The paradox arises that:

> *it is possible that, when he took the standard, he was conscious of having been flogged at school, and that, when made a general, he was conscious of his taking the standard, but had absolutely lost the consciousness of his flogging* (p. 114).

As Reid says, it follows from Locke's theory that the boy is the same person as the young officer, and the officer is the same person as the general, but that the general is not the same person as the boy. But since the transitivity of the identity relation demands that these two be identified as the same person, it seems that Locke is committed to the general both being and not being the same person as the boy.

This argument succeeds against Locke. Contemporary memory-based criteria of identity are designed to counter Reid's objection. They do so by rejecting Locke's restriction to the holding of *direct* memory connections between experiences and their future recall, replacing it with a model of psychological continuity involving overlapping *chains* of memory relations. So if we call the boy, the officer, and the general '*a*,' '*b*,' and '*c*' respectively, then *c* remembers *b's* experience, *b* remembers *a*'s experience, and at all intervening times there is a continuous chain of memory connections sufficient to maintain identity despite the loss of any direct memory connections between *a* and *c*. Such is Parfit's Psychological Criterion, which I will restate in a shorter form:

x (t1) is the same person as *y (t2)* if and only if *x* is psychologically continuous with *y* and with no one else at *t2*.

Clearly this criterion can accommodate such commonplace phenomena as forgetting, since our normal rate of forgetting is not great enough to threaten either of the criterion's two integral relations of psychological continuity or psychological connectedness. It faces a more serious challenge when we consider various forms of amnesia. I will now discuss some forms of organic amnesia (i.e., where there is a known physical cause, as opposed to psychogenic amnesia, where the trouble is psychologically based).

Traumatic amnesia is a common consequence of receiving a severe blow to the head, for example following a road accident. It has three main phases. The first stage is *post-traumatic* amnesia, commencing when the subject first regains consciousness. It is characterized by a general disorientation, of not knowing where one is, what day it is, etc. This is followed by a period of *retrograde* amnesia, in which one's equilibrium becomes more reinstated, but where events prior to the accident cannot be recalled. At first, this amnesia can extend over a period of years, but memories are gradually recovered, although the moments immediately prior to the accident can never be recalled. The common explanation for this is that the information has not been sufficiently consolidated, as the trauma of the accident has interfered with the transfer to long-term storage. The third stage, *anterograde* amnesia, which overlaps the second stage, is characterized by tiredness and difficulties in concentrating, resulting in problems with learning and retaining new information.

THE SLEEPING PILL

Given the limited and temporary nature of traumatic amnesia, one would think that Parfit's Psychological Criterion would not be bothered by it. However, Parfit constructs an argument involving retrograde amnesia to draw some startling conclusions. This occurs in his thought-experiment entitled 'The Sleeping Pill' [1984, p. 287], in which he makes a challenging comparison between the predicaments of the subject of this experiment and that of a Teletransportation scenario. The story begins with the well-acknowledged fact that some sleeping pills can cause retrograde amnesia. Thus I will remain awake for one hour after having taken the pill, but the following day will not remember anything that happened during the half-hour before I fell asleep the previous night. So if I have taken such a pill just over thirty minutes ago, then the person who wakes tomorrow will be psychologically continuous with me as I was before taking he pill, but not with me now. I am, according to Parfit, presently on a 'psychological branchline' that will end when I fall asleep. Until then, I will be psychologically continuous with 'myself-in-the-past,' but not with 'myself-in-the-future.' Thus the relationship between 'me now' and 'me tomorrow' is like my relation to someone else inasmuch as any intentions that I now form will not be acted upon tomorrow, and any bright ideas I now have will be forgotten, unless I resort to public means of communication such as writing myself a note.

Parfit says that this predicament is analogous to a variant on the teletransportation story $T2$ (let us call it '$T2^*$') in which my replica is not created until I die. He suggests that the situations are structurally identical in the sense that if we give the names 'a,' 'b,' and 'c' respectively to, firstly in the sleeping pill case, myself before taking the pill, myself after it has taken effect but while I am still awake, and myself when I wake the following day; and secondly in $T2^*$, respectively to myself before entering the Scanner, myself after the recording of my blueprint, and my replica after my death, then in both cases we have psychological continuity between a and b, and between a and c, but not between b and c.

If Parfit's comparison is correct, then we have a difficult dilemma. Given that in $T2^*$ we do not want to ascribe stages a, b, and c to one same person, then we would be equally barred from doing so in the sleeping pill case, which would be extremely counterintuitive—it is obvious that I am the same person throughout. On the other hand, if we accept this latter conclusion, then we would be bound to do so in $T2^*$, which again is most undesirable.

Andrew Brennan argues that such a dilemma is an illusion, since Parfit is mistaken in comparing the two cases. He analyzes them in terms of his 'survival conditions' (see Chapter 4), arguing that in $T2^*$, a survives both as b and as c, but that b does not survive as c, since b and c are not causally related. However, both b and c are causally related to a; b through physical continuity, and c the result of a copying process using a as the prototype. By contrast, in the sleeping pill case, c's amnesia is causally dependent on events happening to b, as the pill has interfered with the brain's processing functions, so that any experiences occurring at that time cannot later be retrieved by c.

Brennan is correct in pointing out the asymmetry between the two cases. However, it seems to me that his analysis of the sleeping pill case, despite its intrinsic merits, has moved away from anything that can be understood in terms of a Psychological Criterion since, if it were to be elaborated upon, it would be in the language of neuroscience and pharmacology. This is no problem for me, but it may be for Parfit.

Another way of dealing with retrograde amnesia in the sleeping pill case is just to say that the Psychological Criterion is loose enough to accommodate such lapses in memory, since psychological continuity still holds to a sufficient degree to maintain identity, given the continuity between a and c. This position is strengthened considerably when we reject the privileged status of memory-connections within the Psychological Criterion, and widen it to include such factors as consistency of character, of likes and dislikes, the continued ability to use language and to perform practical skills, all of which are unaffected by retrograde amnesia.

VARIETIES OF MEMORY

I keep stressing the need to discuss memory, and therefore any Psychological Criterion, in terms of a far richer conceptual scheme than has usually been employed. Far too often, we have followed Locke & Co. in taking a unitary view of memory. However, memory comprises a number of interconnecting systems, each with a different specialized function, but cooperating in the task of storing information for future use. All talk of someone 'losing his memory' is misleading, since it tacitly assumes this false unitary model. Amnesic syndrome does not involve a general or overall loss of memory, nor a general deterioration in memory function, but rather a variety of possible selective impairments, in which some systems can be severely damaged while others are relatively unaffected.

The following discussion of severe cases of organic amnesia will employ the well-known distinction between long-term and short-term storage. 'Long-term storage' refers to all information stored such that it is potentially retrievable over times greater than a few seconds. 'Short-term storage' comprises the set of systems facilitating the temporary storage of information required to perform another more inclusive mental operation. For example, mental arithmetic requires the temporary storage of numbers that can be retrieved at the appropriate stage of the operation, after which they can be discarded. Likewise, in understanding a sentence one needs to be able to remember the first words in the sentence when the last words are being spoken or read.

Organic amnesia is caused by damage to the limbic system of the brain, usually involving the temporal lobes of the cortex, the hippocampus, and mamillary bodies. Causes include viruses, stroke, brain tumor, and Korsakoff syndrome, which I will now discuss. Korsakoff syndrome is a result of chronic alcoholism and subsequent thiamine (vitamin B1) deficiency. One problem in ascertaining the degree of amnesia suffered in such cases is that the syndrome is usually accompanied by other more general intellectual and cognitive impairments. However, some memory systems remain intact. Short-term storage is usually unaffected, as are lin-

'or skills. Such patients retain *semantic*
..nowledge, but this can be restricted to
..i before the onset of the disease. For example
..ous reported cases in which, when the patient is
..s the current President, will reply "JFK," i.e., whoever
..sident at the time before amnesia took hold. This peculiar
..ation is due to the fact that Korsakoff patients have great difficulty in learning (and therefore in remembering) any new information. Thus they suffer from both anterograde and retrograde
amnesia.

Korsakoff patients show some degree of residual learning capacity, which shows that *procedural* memory (i.e., information in
long-term storage concerning complex skills that can only be given
a partial description, e.g., riding a bicycle) is not fully destroyed.
Such patients can also retain the ability to perform various tasks
and skills that they acquired prior to the disease.

The other major area of disfunction in Korsakoff Syndrome is in
episodic memory, i.e., 'autobiographical memory,' the ability to
remember past experiences from the inside. Again, this can remain
intact for periods prior to the onset of the disease. Thus, a patient
may retain vivid memories of his youth, to the extent that he may
believe himself to still be that age. However, vast quantities of his
past will be lost to him. For example, if you were to meet an
extreme Korsakoff patient for the first time one morning, and
returned that afternoon, he may not recognize you, nor remember
having met anyone that morning. It is therefore understandable that
such patients are not aware that there is anything wrong with
them—how could an amnesic remember that he couldn't remember? Perhaps this is a blessing. Two case histories, from Oliver
Sacks, will serve to display the horror of such a predicament.

TWO CASE HISTORIES

Jimmie G. suffered from severe retrograde amnesia due to
Korsakoff syndrome. When Sacks first met him in 1975, Jimmie
thought that the year was 1945, and that he was still nineteen years

of age. When Sacks confronted him with his mirror image and asked if the middle-aged man reflected there could be a youth of nineteen, Jimmie went into a blind uncomprehending panic which, perhaps mercifully, was extremely shortlived, since the experience was forgotten in a few seconds once his attention was distracted. In general, he had no sense of the passing of time. As Sacks observed, "He is a man without a past, stuck in a constantly changing, meaningless moment" (p. 28). On being interviewed at the hospital where he had resided for many years, he asked of Sacks, "What is this place, Doc? Do I work here?" He possessed no semantic nor episodic memory concerning anything after 1945. Beyond this date there was no certainty, and he was left with only guesses, instantly forgotten, to try to make sense of his situation. Sacks recalled Hume's account of the inner life of man as essentially comprising "a bundle or collection of perceptions, which succeed each other with an inconceivable rapidity, and are in perpetual flux and movement" (Bk. 1, ch. 4, p. 6), and ruefully reflected that such a picture is realized not by people in general, but in such damaged cases as Jimmie G, the 'Humean being.'

William Thompson is an even more extreme case of Korsakoff syndrome. Unlike Jimmie, he cannot recall any part of his life, nor has knowledge of any facts. He has no idea who he is, adopting and casting personae aside rapidly and randomly. Likewise, he will see any other person addressing him as being up to a dozen different people in the space of five minutes, moving from one construction to another, unaware of any discontinuity, and delivering each 'version of reality' with equal force. In fact, each of these conflicting accounts were equal in value to him (i.e., virtually valueless), and such basic distinctions as true/false, real/unreal, relevant/irrelevant, important/trivial cease to apply in his ontology. To quote Sacks, "For him they were not fictions, but how he suddenly saw or interpreted the world... its radical flux or incoherence could not be tolerated, acknowledged for an instance" (p. 104). He could not see anything wrong with himself, precisely because he was lacking any stable viewpoint or perspective from which to make such a judgment. In his state of permanent Korsakoff psychosis, he was "continually creating a world and a self... such a patient must literally make himself (and his world) up at every moment" (p. 105).

Do these tragic cases present serious problems for Parfit's criterion? Let us first examine the relation of psychological connectedness. Since short-term storage remains intact, one could say that most Korsakoff patients possess a fair degree of psychological connectedness in the extremely short term, i.e., moment to moment, although even this may be denied in the case of William Thompson. By Parfit's definition (see Chapter 1), this connectedness would hold only to a very low degree, well below that of the 'strong connectedness' that requires that at least half the direct psychological connections be retained into the following day. This condition would definitely rule out William Thompson. In the case of Jimmie G, one could argue for psychological continuity on the basis of his well-established memories of events and experiences prior to 1945. It would be impossible to decide if these memory connections are sufficient to maintain his identity, since we do not have strict criteria for counting memory connections. However, if we broaden the Psychological Criterion as I have suggested above, and include such factors as continuity of character, of tastes, of values, then Jimmie is seen as possessing a far higher degree of psychological continuity than previously judged. The need to expand the Psychological Criterion becomes even clearer when we consider the tragic case of Clive Wearing, the subject of a British documentary entitled 'Prisoner of Consciousness.' (Parts of this program were broadcast in the United States in the PBS series 'The Mind.') Clive's amnesia was caused by a viral infection that damaged the frontal and temporal lobes of his brain. As with those afflicted with Korsakoff syndrome, Clive's procedural memory remains relatively intact despite an episodic memory so devastated that he is unable to remember anything that happened more than a few moments previously. Still, he remains an accomplished musician, and continues to read music, to play, arrange and conduct just as before. His predicament was dramatically illustrated when he was invited to play and conduct a choir in a church in which he had regularly performed in the past. He protested vehemently that he had never seen any of it before in his life, since (as he constantly insisted, he was only conscious, *for the first time,* at that present moment). While angrily protesting that he'd never played any musical instrument before, he was placed in front of the keyboard, and was amazed when the music began to flow from his fingers. In addition to this continuity of procedural memory, Clive's character remained constant (or as constant as it could be said to be, under the circumstances). In particular, the most noticeable constant in his life was his love for his wife, despite his tragicomic greeting of her 'for the first time' each time she entered the room. When we take all this into account, Clive's psychological continuity is far higher than it seemed when our view was restricted to episodic memory. This approach gains support from the testimony of Clive Wearing's wife, who stated that, throughout her husband's illness, "I've never lost touch with the 'Cliveness' of Clive... his soul, his person is unchanged... he's still the same man." I understand her to be pointing at least in part to the forms of continuity I have mentioned. However, even after all this, William Thompson still fails to make the grade, as the flux equally extends to these newly included aspects of mental life. He cannot with any accuracy be said to even have a personality, likes and dislikes, opinions, values, etc., as such concepts assume an underlying consistency that he does not possess. He cannot even be said to have a *self* (in the sense that I shall develop in the final two chapters). So even my broadened Psychological Criterion fails to accommodate him. Sadly, he has ceased to be a person.

Let us return to the beginning of the chapter, to Flew's distinction between the logical and factual senses of 'can.' regarding the ability to remember past experiences. We saw that neither usage could provide a satisfactory criterion of personal identity within a Lockean framework. Flew was mistaken in assuming that he had exhausted the possibilities. However, what we need is the sense of 'can' that limits what is *theoretically* possible, in the sense described in Chapter 5. We need an account of how memory works, including an explanation of when and how these functions break down. The introduction of 'theoretical possibility' forces us to ask fundamental questions regarding what a criterion of personal identity is, and what it is for. From Locke through to the present day, various formulations of the Psychological Criterion are located in terms of their opposition to a Physical Criterion. This conflict developed because it was considered 'possible' that the two criteria could diverge and provide different answers to questions of identity. Hence it was a very real question as to which Criterion was correct or had primacy. But if such a divergence is not theoretically possible, then this whole enterprise has been one long red herring.

APPENDIX: PSYCHOGENIC FUGUE

However, matters are more complicated in the case of psychogenic fugue, a condition that acts as a 'bridge' between the amnesic disorders discussed in this chapter and the dissociative disorders to be discussed in Chapter 8. In psychogenic fugue, a person typically disappears, wandering far from home for days or weeks on end, during which he has no recall of his life before his flight. That is, he suffers a complete temporary loss of episodic memory, while being unaware of this loss. Such fugues typically end as suddenly as they began, with the person 'snapping out of it,' often on waking from sleep, with the memories of his life prior to the fugue fully restored, but those of his life during the fugue state now inaccessible.

William James describes a typical case of psychogenic fugue, wherein one Rev. Ansel Bourne disappeared from his home in Providence, Rhode Island, on January 20, 1887. Nothing was discovered concerning his whereabouts until March 14 when, in Norristown, Pennsylvania, one A.J. Brown, who had arrived in town six weeks before and opened a general store, awoke one night in panic, having recognized himself as Ansel Bourne. He had no knowledge of where he was, how he had got there, nor what he had been doing there. He remembered nothing about the previous few weeks in Norristown 'as' A.J. Brown. The last thing he recalled was withdrawing money from the bank in Providence on January 20.

Three years later, William James attempted to retrieve these lost memories using hypnosis. However, when Bourne recalled them while hypnotized, he, 'as Brown,' confessed only vague knowledge of Ansel Bourne, being unsure whether they had ever met. James confessed that "I had hoped by suggestion, etc. to run these two personalities into one, and make these memories continuous, but no artifice would avail to accomplish this, and Mr Bourne's skull today covers two distinct personal selves" (p. 393).

In Chapter 8, I will investigate whether any literal, non-metaphorical sense can be made of James' claim that the man before him comprises two distinct selves. This will lead me to enquire into the fundamental concept of 'unity of mind.' This is also the central issue of the following chapter, regarding the implications of split-brain research.

CHAPTER SEVEN

COMMISSUROTOMY AND THE UNITY OF MIND

INTRODUCTION

S plit-brain research, i.e., investigations into the consequences of commissurotomy, has been recognized as having profound and far-reaching implications for the study of personal identity and for the central concept of 'unity of mind.' In particular, the whole issue of synchronic identity, resting on a notion of 'psychological unity-at-a-time,' has been called into question by these experimental findings.

In this chapter I will challenge the widely held view that split-brain patients have 'two minds' and are thus two distinct persons in one body. In place of the 'unity' of mind, I will make a distinction between the *singularity* of mind and the *integration* of mind. I emphasize that 'a single mind' is not hypothesized in order to explain mental integration, but is merely a mark that coherence holds to a satisfactory degree. I will argue that there is no strict demarcation line regarding what counts as a single mind, and that mental coherence is always a matter of degree (whether in the case of ourselves, or of split-brain patients). I conclude that our concept of a single mind can accommodate split-brain phenomena.

One of the most noticeable recent developments in philosophical studies of personal identity has been the convergence of the two traditionally opposing theories, the Physical Criterion and the Psychological Criterion, due to their common acknowledgement of the significance of the brain. Supporters of the Physical Criterion regard the brain as the one organ that one absolutely cannot lose and yet remain the same person. They assume that it is a condition of the holding of identity for a physical object that there be an unbroken spatio-temporal path connecting all its 'stages,' and, in the case of human beings, the essential 'traveller' along this path is the brain. In other words, I go where my brain goes. I can lose my hair, my teeth, my arms, my heart, lungs and liver, yet still remain me—everything except my brain. Thus it was argued that if *a*'s brain were transplanted into *b*'s body, the resulting person would be *a*, and the operation would be more accurately described not as *b* having a brain transplant, but as *a* having a body transplant, with this being merely the limit to cases of organ transplant. For their part, supporters of the Psychological Criterion conferred special status on the brain as being the physical means whereby all psychological phenomena, notably memory, were realized.

All such discussions assumed that the brain was the *indivisible* bearer of consciousness and of selfhood. In other words, it was taken for granted that the functional integrity of the brain could not withstand division nor substantial diminution, and that no less than a complete and fully operative brain could succeed in embodying a full human consciousness. However, once more detailed knowledge of the brain was acquired, this assumption began to be undermined. In Nagel's [1971] words, it began to look possible that the idea of a single person, and of a single subject of experience "may resist the sort of coordination with an understanding of humans as physical systems, that would be necessary to yield anything describable as an understanding of the physical basis of mind" (p. 147).

COMMISSUROTOMY DESCRIBED

'Split-brain surgery' is something of a misnomer, smacking slightly of journalese. It refers to commissurotomy that, strictly speaking, does not result in the bisection of brains (as many parts of the brain remain intact following the operation) but of the cerebral cortex.

There are various forms of commissurotomy, all involving the cutting of the corpus callosum (literally 'thick-skinned body'), a large transverse band consisting of around 800 million nerve fibres, which directly connects the cerebral hemispheres, thus facilitating direct communication between them. In a *complete* commissurotomy, the entire corpus callosum is sectioned, along with the underlying hippocampal commissure, the fornix, the anterior commissure, and the massa intermedia of the thalamus. This results in the division of the cerebral cortex, with the hemispheres being connected only indirectly via the brain stem and subcortical routes, and thus causing the splitting in sensory and motor functions to be discussed shortly.

A *central* commissurotomy involves the severing of the corpus callosum and the hippocampal commissure, resulting in a tactile but not a visual split. A *frontal* commissurotomy involves the sectioning of the anterior portion of the corpus callosum, the anterior commissure, and the fornix, and results in relatively little splitting of functions, even under experimental conditions.

Complete commissurotomies are rare at present. Modern scanning equipment can precisely locate the source of the epileptic seizure that warrants the operation, and thus we only need section the part of the corpus callosum that would relay the discharge to the other hemisphere. However, complete commissurotomy was the common form of the operation for some time, and has been the focus of most philosophical interest. Accordingly, except where otherwise stated, I will use the term 'commissurotomy' to refer to the operation in its complete form. I will, however, return to the more limited forms, as they will be crucial evidence for my final assessment of the philosophical implications of split-brain research.

Commissurotomy was introduced in the 1940s as a drastic measure to control grand mal epileptic seizures, which originate as an electrical disturbance in a particular site on the cortex, spreading across it to the other hemisphere via the corpus callosum. Since the disturbance increases in magnitude as it proceeds, the idea behind the operation was that by cutting the corpus callosum, the disturbance would not only be limited to its hemisphere of origin, but its magnitude would thereby be severely curtailed. In this respect the operation proved to be successful beyond all expectation, as attacks not only became less severe, but also less common, and in some cases disappeared completely.

Despite the operation's undoubted success regarding epilepsy, it was discovered in time to have some peculiar consequences, which I discuss below. However, these side effects were not immediately apparent. Much of the literature tends to exaggerate the cognitive and behavioral consequences of commissurotomy, understandably concentrating on anomalies. Rather, the fact is that such patients' behavior appears, both to the patients and to observers, to be virtually unaffected most of the time. Indeed, close investigation by clinical researchers at the time revealed no peculiar results. This led many neurologists of the day to ascribe only a minor role if any to the corpus callosum in brain function. One wit suggested that it was only there to transmit epileptic seizures between cerebral hemispheres.

By the 1960s it was discovered that under certain controlled experimental conditions, the response of split-brain patients was highly unusual and alarming in its implications. Specifically, when sensory input was restricted to one hemisphere alone, and a response to this stimulus requested of it, it appeared, in Sperry's [1968a] words, that such patients possessed "two separate spheres of conscious awareness, two separate conscious entities or minds running in parallel in the same cranium, each with its own sensations, perceptions, cognitive processes, learning experiences, memories, and so on" (p. 318).

However, despite a misleading gloss of unanimity that is often presented by neuroscientists and philosophers on these subjects, it must be kept in mind that patients' responses were by no means uniform, even under the most controlled conditions. Large differences in performance have been recorded between different patients, and also in the same patient over a period of time, especially when comparing recent postoperative responses with those of a few years later, when a marked improvement was frequently noted. It seems that eventually some direct communication can be reestablished between disconnected hemispheres. I will return to this fact later on, but for the moment I will confine the discussion to cases that suggest, prima facie, that the operation has resulted in two separate minds in one body. To investigate these cases, we need to be acquainted with the ways in which sensory stimuli are transmitted in a normal brain.

THE EXPERIMENTAL BACKGROUND

Tactile stimuli originating in a given side of the body are transmitted to the cerebral hemisphere on the other side (i.e., contralaterally), except stimuli to the head and neck, which are directly transmitted to both hemispheres.

With visual stimuli, the retina is functionally subdivided so that the left side of both retinae, scanning the right side of the visual field, send impulses to the left hemisphere. Conversely the right halves of both retinae, scanning the left half of the visual field, send impulses to the right hemisphere.

Auditory impulses from either ear are transmitted to both hemispheres, with the signal to the contralateral hemisphere being the stronger.

Olfactory impulses are only transmitted ipsilaterally, i.e., each nostril sends impulses to the hemisphere on its own side of the body.

With motor control, each hemisphere controls the movements of the opposite side of the body, except head and neck movements, which are controlled by both hemispheres together. Each hemisphere has some small degree of ipsilateral control of the body, but this is negligible compared to the other's contralateral control, and is overruled by it in normal brains. However, this ipsilateral control should not be dismissed as being an inevitably small and insignificant facility under all circumstances. It comes into its own in cases where the contralateral hemisphere has been removed or significantly damaged, e.g., by a stroke. Under such circumstances the remaining hemisphere can be trained to develop greater and more refined ipsilateral control. A similar development has been observed in some cases of commissurotomy, with a gradual but significant improvement in ipsilateral control being developed in the years following the operation. In general, it appears that the brain's ability to adapt and take on the functions usually assigned to missing or inoperative structures is at its strongest in children, tending to decrease with age.

In the vast majority of people, the areas of the brain most responsible for language-related functions are located mainly in the left hemisphere—i.e., the left is the *dominant* hemisphere. Thus, should someone suffer a stroke affecting the left hemisphere, he will be left speechless and with vastly impaired linguistic comprehension, although some can be gradually retrieved by means of the right hemisphere. Many left-handed people have their linguistic functions located primarily in the right hemisphere, and there is also a small percentage of people in whom these functions are spread evenly between both hemispheres.

I will now describe some of the experiments performed on split-brain patients, during which the controversial responses were discovered. The patient is seated in front of a blank screen, onto which a tachistoscope flashes signals to a particular side. The patient is asked to stare at a spot in the center of the screen, ensuring that his head and neck movements are minimized. These procedures ensure that the signals are only directly accessible to one hemisphere. The signals are flashed for 200 milliseconds, just long enough for them to be registered by one half of the retinae (corresponding to the half of the visual field onto which the signal was flashed), but not long enough to allow any saccadic eye movements that would bring the signal within the range of the other halves of the retinae and therefore accessed to the other hemisphere. These signals can take the form of words, simple images of familiar objects, or small patches of color. In this last case, two easily distinguishable colors are used—e.g., red and green make an ideal pair, as opposed to red and orange. Each of these colored patches is restricted to half the visual field so that, e.g., the left hemisphere has direct access to the red patch only, and the right hemisphere has access to the green patch only. In such a case, the left hemisphere cannot be directly aware of the color flashed to the right hemisphere, and vice versa.

In the majority of cases, where the left hemisphere is dominant, colors flashed to the right of the screen can be reported verbally, but not colors flashed to the left of the screen, since the right hemisphere is mute. Similar results apply when words are flashed to the respective sides of the screen, and in cases where objects are touched, unseen, by the hands: when the object is held in the right hand, the patient can verbally identify it, but not if it is in his left hand.

However if a word, e.g. 'pencil,' is flashed to the left side of the screen, the left hand will pick out a pencil from among a pile of concealed objects, while the patient will claim that he saw nothing. Likewise if two different words, corresponding to different objects, are flashed onto different sides of the screen, then the patient's hands, hidden from him by a curtain, will search through a pile of unseen objects, seemingly oblivious to the other and its search, until they locate their respective targets.

Another set of experiments, by Levy, Trevarthan, and Sperry, used composite or 'chimeric' imagery: while the patient continued to look straight ahead at the midpoint of the screen as before, a composite image of two half-faces (the left side of one face and the right side of another) was flashed upon a vertical axis of the midpoint of the screen so that each hemisphere only had direct access to one half-face. When asked to *verbally* indicate what image was seen, patients would report seeing the one sent to the left hemisphere. However, when asked to *point* to the one seen, they chose the one sent to the right hemisphere. One further, unexplained oddity was that in both cases the patient would report seeing whole faces. Somehow each hemisphere managed to complete the partial image into the more familiar whole form.

MINDS, BRAINS, AND PERSONS

As Wilkes [1978] argues, when theorists say that these results show split-brain patients to have two distinct minds, they assume that to deny this would lead to contradiction, e.g., to say that some person at time t both knows and does not know some proposition p, or both sees and does not see some object q, etc. Given that the experiments seem to provide cases where the left hemisphere knows that p and that simultaneously the right hemisphere does not know that p, such theorists conclude that the left and right hemispheres must logically constitute two minds, two subjects of experience.

Certainly we feel tempted to say that such patients have two of *something...* but to go further raises problems. As Patricia Churchland says, folk-psychological concepts such as 'mind,' 'self,' and 'center of consciousness' are so vague and theoretically undefined that we don't have clear rules for counting them, since we don't exactly know *what* we are counting. As with other conditions such as Multiple Personality Disorder, alexia, and visual agnosia, these prescientific mentalistic concepts are unable to provide an adequate explanation, or even description, of such conditions. However, it is instructive to draw out the confusions that result from such attempts, and therefore to question the privilege of some of our deepest assumptions about the mind.

As I elaborate in the following chapter, when we attribute 'a single mind' to someone, we are not positing the existence of some entity that explains the coherence of one's mental life. Rather, the attribution of a single mind is another way of saying that such coherence holds to a significant degree. This is in line with the Reductionist thesis 2 (see Chapter 1), that a person consists in a body that undergoes various physical and mental states—i.e., a mind is not something over and above the existence of mental states. However, when we try to specify the minimum degree of coherence required to constitute a single mind, we realize that there is no black-and-white dividing line (as Reductionist thesis 5 elaborates). Still, we can offer paradigm cases that would definitely count as one mind, and others that are more problematic.

Before returning to the main body of experiments regarding split-brain patients, I wish to briefly comment on a couple of cases of 'mental division' that are not sufficient to warrant the ascription of two minds.

One of the peculiar side effects of commissurotomy that was occasionally displayed in nonexperimental settings was the simultaneous manifestation of two sharply conflicting emotions. It seemed as if the two disconnected hemispheres were in opposition, as in the famous case of the man who embraced his wife with one hand while pushing her away with the other. Gillett comments that "it would be implausible... to claim that one of the hemispheres loved his wife and the other one hated her" (p. 227). Gillett seems to think that this would involve a category mistake. However, it is no more peculiar than to say, regarding someone with an intact cortex, that his brain loved his wife. Certainly we tend not to attribute emotions or attitudes to brains or to half-brains, but to persons. However, given the inadequacy of our mentalistic concepts in dealing with these anomalous cases, perhaps we can make such ascriptions here, since we lack a fully appropriate way to describe what is going on.

This form of expression has the merit of highlighting the obvious emotional conflict. However, we can all experience simultaneous conflicting emotions without our mental unity being called into question. We have all felt attracted to and repelled by someone or something at the same time. In fact, this apparent conflict often involves no contradiction, but involves a pair of desires that are not mutually exclusive. For example, perhaps this man had two different responses to different factors relating to his wife. If so, the only difference between his attitudes and our own is the peculiar and extreme way in which his internal conflict was revealed.

My second example involves an experience of my own. I had to make a phone call, so I located the number in the book, closed the book, and began to dial. Once I had reached the third digit of the number, I realized that I could not recall the whole number to myself, i.e., I could not inwardly recite it, nor form a mental picture of it. However, my finger continued to dial 'as if it knew what it was doing,' and I felt that I somehow knew the number. While I could not manifest this knowledge by uttering the number, I could do so by the very act of dialing it—and it turned out that I had dialled correctly.

It is no real help to say that 'my body knew the number, but my mind didn't.' Such a description would leave the nature of these 'knowings' totally open, and thus nothing is explained. A better way to describe what is going on is to appeal to different *types* of knowledge, e.g., between 'knowing how' and 'knowing that,' where I knew the number in the former way but not the latter way (like Clive Wearing at the keyboard). This would avoid the seeming contradiction of 'both knowing and not knowing that p.' No doubt, a complete neuroscience would enable us to describe the processes by which both cognitive modes were realized in an *impersonal* way, without reference to any single subject of experience (see Reductionist thesis 4). Again, this would dissolve any appearance of contradiction.

Having dealt with these side issues, I will now return to the main body of experiments on split-brain patients. One of the first things that any theorist must account for is the divergence between, firstly, patients' seemingly perfectly integrated behavior under virtually all normal conditions (which would seem to encourage the attribution of a single mind); and secondly, the results of controlled experiments like those previously described, which have been cited as grounds for saying that such a unity has been breached, and that patients therefore have two separate minds.

PUCCETTI'S 'TWO PERSON' THEORY

There has been a wide range of responses to these experimental results. By far the most extreme has been from Puccetti [1973], who sees the data as providing grounds for the claim that *all* human beings have two minds, and consist of two persons cohabiting a single body. He offers several arguments to support this truly bizarre claim. Firstly, he asks:

How could commissurotomy create two minds or persons if there was just one before? Which mind—the left-based one or the right-based one—is brand new? And how are we to make a choice here? Both brains...were conscious and functioning in their rather specialized way before the operation. It is just that they functioned more synchronously—because of the commissural connections—and no longer do so in test situations...thus even in the normal cerebrally intact human being there must be two persons (p. 351).

So he is saying that the fact that our two 'minds' are connected by the corpus callosum will not significantly alter their functioning, except in making a little more information available to them.

He backs up his case by pointing to cases of hemispherectomy, wherein:

> *the same personality, character traits, and long-term memory traces persist postoperatively. The only way I can see to explain this is to say that the same "person" did not survive hemispherectomy at all. Because this former "person" was never a unitary person at all. He or she was a compound of two persons who functioned in concert by trans-commissural exchange—what has survived is one of two very similar persons with roughly parallel memory traces, nearly synchronized emotional states, perceptual experiences, and so on, but different processing functions* (p. 352).

However, the results of hemispherectomy do not point unequivocally to the conclusion that two minds existed prior to the operation. We must distinguish two conclusions:

1. Prior to hemispherectomy, there existed two separate but synchronized minds in one body.

2. Prior to hemispherectomy, there existed one mind that had the *potential* to constitute two separate minds.

Only the second conclusion is justified by the facts. And given the high degree of redundancy in the neural structures embodying such a mind, we should not find this conclusion so shocking. It only looks counterintuitive when we fall into the trap of reifying the mind, and seeing it as some 'thing' over and above our mental states, in opposition to Reductionist theses 2 & 3.

Puccetti's criterion for the individuation of minds is unclear. He would surely accept that information is directly exchanged between the hemispheres by means of the corpus callosum, and therefore that the cerebral cortex functions as one integrated system (within a larger system). He must then acknowledge that a person can have an overall integrative awareness of simultaneously having two mental states (e.g., thinking about lunch while listening to music) whose neural embodiments are located over both hemi-spheres. Given this, it is hard to see how he can count two distinct minds without begging the question by reifying minds on a hemi-spherical model.

Before moving on, we can quickly dispose of a false compromise that attempts to compatibilize divergent results by the thesis that split-brain patients have one mind under normal circumstances and two minds under experimental conditions. This is an entirely ad hoc move with no explanatory force, and encouraging no independent grounds for support. It also has the untenable implication that the number of minds present is determined by something completely external to the patient. Also, as Nagel says:

There is nothing about the experimental situation that might be expected to produce a fundamental internal change in the patient. In fact it pro-duces no anatomical changes and merely elicits a noteworthy set of symp-toms. So unusual an event as a mind's popping in and out of existence would have to be explained by something more than its explanatory conve-nience (p. 161).

COGNITION IN THE RIGHT HEMISPHERE

One is not likely to sustain a telling argument to the effect that the right hemisphere does not deserve to be regarded as a mind because the left is dominant. Such a position is held by Sir John Eccles, who writes of the "uniqueness and exclusiveness of the dominant hemi-sphere in respect of conscious experience." However, the inability to produce linguistic signs is no proof of the absence of conscious experience, as such a claim would reduce pre-verbal children to the level of automata. Likewise, as Puccetti observes, "if speech is a necessary condition of consciousness, then the aphasic who can play piano—as Ravel did—is playing unconsciously" (p. 342). Also, one need only become acquainted with the modes of cogni-tion associated with the right hemisphere, and their degree of com-plexity, to see the untenability of Eccles' view. As Nagel says:

There seems no reason in principle to regard verbalizability as a neces-sary condition of consciousness... what the right hemisphere can do on its own is too elaborate, too intentionally directed and too psychologically intelligible to be regarded merely as a collection of unconscious respons-es... the right hemisphere follows instructions, integrates tactile, auditory and visual stimuli, and does most of the things a good mind should do (p. 156).

If one is still in any doubt over the legitimacy of calling the right hemisphere conscious, one need only be reminded of its ability to adapt and take over functions that had been in the province of the left hemisphere, in cases where the left has been removed or is largely incapacitated. It has been suggested that in normal conditions the left hemisphere inhibits the right's latent linguistic abilities, and that these controls are removed in cases of left-hemi-spherectomy or strokes affecting the left hemisphere.

Numerous studies, both popular and scholarly, have been pub-lished describing the different but complementary modes of cogni-tion typical of the two hemispheres. Indeed, some of this information has filtered down to the general public. How many times has someone described himself or herself to you as being "a right-brain person" or suchlike? For light relief, I reproduce one of the most extensive categorizations, by Joseph Bogen (in Campbell), a pioneer of split-brain research:

LEFT	RIGHT
intellect	intuition
convergent	divergent
intellectual	sensuous
deductive	imaginative
active	receptive
discrete	continuous
abstract	concrete
realistic	impulsive
propositional	imaginative
transformational	associative
lineal	nonlineal

historical   timeless
explicit   tacit
objective   subjective

Looking at this list of complementary-opposite pairs, I am inclined to suspect that Dr. Bogen received a Thesaurus for Christmas, as it repeats and elaborates on a couple of general distinctions by means of near-synonyms and associated concepts. Rather than talking in such terms, it is perhaps safer to stick to descriptions of what the respective hemispheres can actually do.

So Eccles' claim that the right hemisphere is incapable of conscious experience most certainly underestimates its abilities. In fairness to him, this view was once widely held, and seemed plausible. In recent times, experimental results have suggested that the right hemisphere has more language-related abilities than had been previously realized. In the 1960s, various tests by Gazzaniga and Sperry showed that in split-brain patients, the right hemisphere could not initiate a verbal response to questions regarding sensory stimuli that had been exposed to it alone. This left it open whether the hemisphere merely lacked motor control to allow speech, or whether there was a more general lack of capacity for linguistic understanding. Later tests indicated that it had some limited linguistic comprehension, e.g., it could match simple concrete nouns with pictures, but could not do this with complex nouns or verbs. It also seemed oblivious to syntactical distinctions. Also, when a verbal command was given, the left hand could retrieve the relevant object, whether it was asked for directly, or by means of simple clues, such as "What do monkeys eat a lot of?", to which a banana was retrieved.

In the mid 1970s, Zaidel devised a set of experiments to see whether the right hemisphere's linguistic comprehension improved if images of words were presented for longer time intervals than tachistoscopic techniques allowed. He designed a 'Z-lens,' a special type of contact lens that blocked light to the left-half of each retina. Given more time to scan the words, the right hemisphere displayed what Zaidel estimated to be the level of linguistic comprehension of a ten-year old—a vast improvement on previous findings. This led theorists to consider whether the question of the lateralization of linguistic functions was not more complex than was previously realized, with the right hemisphere being capable of significant contributions to at least some of the aspects concerned. However, as before, there is a frustrating lack of unity in experimental results. Zaidel's estimate was based on the performance of just two patients, with another four showing negligible right-hemispherical linguistic comprehension. Likewise, in Gazzaniga's earlier experiments, only three out of twenty-eight showed any significant level of linguistic ability. All this indicates that research still has a long way to go before definitive theories can be presented.

Larry DeWitt attempts a softer version of Eccles' theory. He allows that the right hemisphere is conscious, and that it thus qualifies as a mind, but lacks the particularly reflexive consciousness required to count as a self. In other words, it lacks self-consciousness, the ability to think of oneself as oneself:

At the lowest level, we have 'consciousness,' the basic phenomenal awareness that accompanies acts of perceptions, emotions, sensations: in order to possess a 'mind,' the organism must possess a hierarchical ordering of behavioral priorities which are consciously utilized in intentional actions;... by 'consciousness of self,' I mean the ability to apprehend oneself as being distinct from other similar beings, to recognize one's actions and thoughts as belonging in some sense to oneself (p. 42).

DeWitt says that the right hemisphere lacks this self-consciousness, which he links with the ability to use language. He cites experiments in presenting chimps with their mirror images, whereupon they gradually cease to regard these images as being of other animals, but rather to be somehow associated with themselves, which would seem to require the grasp of a rudimentary self-consciousness. DeWitt sees the significance of such a testing procedure as in providing a way to check for the existence of self-consciousness without the need for verbal communication. He conjectures that a similar test would prove that the human right hemisphere lacks any self-consciousness.

Puccetti [1975] replies that DeWitt errs in running together the ability to initiate verbal responses with the ability to understand language, and argues that Zaidel's tests show that the right hemisphere possesses this latter ability. He also cites Sperry's experiments wherein the right hemisphere responds to a verbal request, such as 'draw the figure you see using your left hand,' where the image of a dollar sign is restricted to the right hemisphere and the image of a question mark is restricted to the left. The patient is asked to draw what he sees with his left hand (which is hidden from view) and, as he draws, is asked to describe what he is drawing. The patient said that he was drawing a question mark, whereas he was drawing a dollar sign.

Puccetti takes up DeWitt's challenge, saying that an experiment could be devised wherein tachistoscopic images could be flashed exclusively to the right hemisphere, and the patient asked to press a button with his left hand upon seeing images of his own face. Puccetti conjectures that the right hemisphere would actually do better than the left, since the right is known to be superior in facial recognition, and since failure to recognize faces (including one's own) is always found to be due to a lesion in the right parietal lobe. In fact, such experiments were performed by Sperry and Zaidel and, while the results vindicated Puccetti to some extent, they were inconclusive. Basically, when the patient's visual image was flashed, there was no immediate recognition. This only came gradually, e.g., "I don't know...yes, it might be me...it is me...yes, definitely." The researchers put this down to the assistance of verbal signals from the left hemisphere. So the results indicate that while the right hemisphere has some sense of self, this cannot be accurately quantified, nor how it compares to that of the left. A more crucial reservation is that the results show merely that the right recognizes *a* self, not that it recognizes itself as itself as distinct from the left hemisphere.

SPERRY'S 'TWO MIND' THEORY

I will now turn to the view, originally associated with the neuroscientist Roger Sperry, that split-brain patients, unlike the rest of us, always have two distinct centers of consciousness, both in every-day life and under experimental conditions. The most obvious problem facing this theory is to account for the high degree of inte-grated behavior seemingly exhibited by such patients under normal circumstances. This can be explained quite easily. Take the case of vision: saccadic eye movement causes an image to be registered on both halves of the retina within around 250 milliseconds, thus enabling both hemispheres to gain direct access to the same stim-uli. This, plus head and neck movement, can explain how both hemispheres will gather virtually identical information regarding all but instantaneous features of the world. Thus under normal cir-cumstances, split-brain patients will exhibit nothing indicating a split or a plurality in consciousness. This does not refute the claim that they have a continually divided consciousness, since we can conclude that they do not have a single stream of conscious experi-ences, but two parallel streams, due to the independent duplication of sensory stimuli, with no direct causal connection between the corresponding mental states—i.e., with two separate causal path-ways from the retinae to their respective hemispheres.

Sperry noted that each hemisphere has *indirect* access to the other's mental contents by means of 'cross-cuing' strategies, whereby one hemisphere uses information deriving from behav-ioral responses originating from the other. This phenomenon was illustrated in experiments by Gazzaniga [1970], designed to test whether the right hemisphere could verbally identify color stimuli. With the image restricted to the right hemisphere, the patient was asked to guess whether red or green had been flashed. Since it was the *left* that was initiating the talking while being blind to the stim-uli, it was assumed that the patient had only a 50% chance of suc-cess. However, researchers noted that a significantly higher rate of success was achieved if the initial guess were allowed to be revised, without the patient being told whether or not it was cor-rect, and a second guess permitted. Yet they were satisfied that they had set up the experiment to prevent the left hemisphere gaining direct access to the stimuli. The clue to what was going on came when they noticed that the patient seemed to know that his initial guess was wrong. Thus if red were flashed, and the first guess was correct, he would be content with this. However if he guessed green he would react immediately, perhaps with a frown or a shake of the head, saying, "No, I meant red." What was happening was that since auditory impulses are transmitted to both hemispheres, and since both hemispheres can activate head and neck movements, the right hemisphere, having heard the left answer "green," and having recognized this as the wrong answer, would react with a disapproving gesture. This would be picked up by the left hemisphere, who would infer that a mistake had been made, and revise the answer, which would then be greeted with a smile.

Similarly if an object is placed, out of sight, in a patient's left hand, when asked to identify it, the patient will usually guess wrongly, since there is only a small and primitive form of ipselateral recognition of tactile stimuli, and since the dominant hemisphere has no direct access to the object. However, as in the previous case, the right hemisphere will hear the left's guess, will then frown, etc., and this will cue the left to revise the guess.

As Sperry would say, cross-cuing alone does not prove that split-brain patients have one single mind. Its use is similar to the way in which we come to know the contents of another person's mind. That is, we have no direct access, but come to it inferentially. With split-brain patients, one hemisphere does not have access to the other's contents in the same way that it has access to its own. It knows its own contents directly and non-inferentially, whereas its knowledge of the other's contents is of the same epistemological status as is its knowledge of the contents of another person's mind.

THE SUBJECTIVE VIEW

I now turn briefly from my main line of argument to consider the subjective side of commissurotomy, i.e., what it's like 'from the inside.' The left hemisphere does not disown actions initiated by the right. Rather, it acts from an unconscious assumption of unity, confabulating and integrating such an action into a comprehensible schema by means of plausible explanations, as if the intention and motive were its own. This tendency to gloss over paradox and the disruption of deep assumptions seems to be irresistible. This integrative impulse persists even when the patient is relatively informed concerning the effects of commissurotomy. For example, Gazzaniga & Ledoux flashed the image of a snowy scene to the right hemisphere, while simultaneously flashing the image of a chicken claw to the left. Each hemisphere was then shown a sequence of pictures, and asked to select the picture that most matched the observed image. The left hand indicated a shovel as linked with the snowy scene, while the right hand indicated a chicken head to match the claw, justifying these choices as "the chicken claw goes with the chicken, and you need a shovel to clean out the chicken shed." Thus, the left hemisphere justified the left-hand choice by integrating it into its own explanatory schema.

Gillett emphasizes this integrative impulse, which he extends to examples in which the patient is conscious of a conflict that he tries to overcome by various means:

Because they do try to reintegrate their information, or make best use of their disrupted brain function in tackling the tasks they are set, they can properly be said to be struggling with certain confusions to which they find themselves rather than to have become two mutually independent streams of consciousness which are in a no more than contingent relation to each other (p. 227).

However, it is worth asking why the patient's own subjective view of his situation should be assumed to have any special or conclusive validity. It may just be a fact about the commissurotomized brain that it cannot help struggling towards a greater integration of experience and action, and regarding itself as a single center of consciousness, but may be radically misled over this, as with amputees who suffer pains in 'phantom limbs.' Once we step outside the language of the neurosciences we are at a loss to describe adequately what is going on, and there is no reason to assume that this confusion is any less marked from the first-person perspective.

SPERRY CHALLENGED

Returning to Sperry, his criterion of a unified mind or consciousness is that its physical basis must enable its constituent brain states to be directly causally connected to each other (i.e., without an external intermediary), so that the corresponding mental states can be co-experienced:

The criterion for unity is an operational one; that is, the right and left components, coalesced through commissural connection, function in brain dynamics as a unit... In the normal brain the right and left hemispheric components combine and function as a unit in the causal sequence of cerebral control. In the divided brain, on the other hand, each hemisphere component gets its own separate causal effect as a distinct entity (Sperry [1968a] p. 298).

This is in agreement with Nagel:

Roughly, we assume that a single mind has sufficiently immediate access to its conscious states that, for elements of experience and other mental events occurring simultaneously or in close temporal proximity, the mind which is their subject can also experience the simpler relations between them if it attends to them (p. 160).

By such a criterion, in split-brain patients the left and right hemispheres cannot constitute the physical basis of one unified consciousness because the cutting of the corpus callosum removes the physical basis of the direct connecting system between them, and thus no direct causal relations can exist between any two brain states located in different hemispheres. They can only be connected indirectly, either via subcortical routes, or via inference from external clues.

This position is a strong one, but not conclusive. Two facts are worth considering: firstly, it is well established that in infancy there is no traffic of information between the hemispheres, as the corpus callosum only becomes functional at around two years of age, and only fully operative at around ten. It is assumed that this slowly evolving process allows the two hemispheres to develop their different modes of cognition with a degree of independence. Secondly, consider people born with asymptomatic agenesis of the corpus callosum—i.e., who never develop a corpus callosum, yet in whom no unusual behavioral or cognitive responses were discovered, neither in normal circumstances nor when exposed to the very tests that elicited the telltale responses in split-brain patients. Given that they responded to these experiments exactly like someone with an intact and functioning corpus callosum, we have no reason to say that they possess a 'divided consciousness' nor 'two minds.'

These latter cases show that an intact corpus callosum is not a necessary condition for possession of a single mind. If so, then the cutting of the corpus callosum does not in itself imply that such patients cannot have a single mind. The current explanation of the functioning of people with asymptomatic agenesis of the corpus callosum is that certain minor commissures have taken on the functions normally carried out by the corpus callosum. This is not considered peculiar, since it is to be expected that the structure of the brain should allow for some degree of adaptability, and we have seen some evidence for a degree of redundancy in design with the independent bipolar duplication of sensory information, and the fairly late development of a fully functioning corpus callosum. In fact it is now believed that the transfer of information across the corpus callosum is highly redundant in the everyday functioning of *normal* brains, being largely filtered out by some information-integrating system within the cortex, and thus playing little role in the integration of mental life. If so, it appears that the integration of behavior in normal brains is largely carried out by the same mechanisms as in split brains, namely bipolar independent duplication of information.

I will now return to the main body of experiments, and construct an ideal experiment that can be used to launch the strongest argument against the view that split-brain patients possess a single mind. The experiment takes the usual form of a test to establish that under the previously described experimental conditions, when patches of red and green are flashed simultaneously to opposite sides of the visual field, each hemisphere will only be aware of one of these colors. The argument is as follows:

1. Take a situation as described above, in which both hemispheres perceive and correctly identify their respective color patches.

2. Red and green are logical contraries, so nothing can be all-red and all-green at the same time.

3. So one subject of experience (i.e., one person with one mind) cannot perceive only red and only green at the same time t.

4. It is logically possible for a subject A to see only red at t, and for a subject B to see only green at t, providing that $A \neq B$.

5. Given that only red and only green were simultaneously perceived at t, it follows that $A \neq B$, i.e., that the left and right hemispheres are separate and distinct subjects of experience at t.

SPLIT BRAINS AND SINGLE MINDS

I will argue that in claiming that split-brain patients have two minds at all times, such 'two-mind theorists' have committed two main errors: Firstly, to argue that the question of the 'unity of mind' or of 'unity of consciousness' is a determinate 'all or nothing' matter; and secondly to reify the mind, and thus to regard 'minds' as things that come in discrete units.

All such talk of 'unity' is guilty of an ambiguity that is at the root of the two-mind theory's error. We must make a distinction between (a) the *singularity* of mind, i.e., the number of minds present; and (b) the *integration* of mind, i.e., the degree of internal coherence or, by contrast, compartmentalization, within a single mind.

Singularity of mind is always an all-or-nothing matter, never a matter of degree. However (as stated in Reductionist thesis 5) there are conceivable cases in which it is an empty question to ask how many minds are present—not because there is some metaphysical indeterminacy in the world regarding this issue, but because the concept of 'mind' may be too vague to allow a definite answer.

However, our concept of 'a single mind' can allow a fair degree of compartmentalization. As Margolis says:

The so-called unity of minds and persons is designed to accommodate all sorts of anomalies—for instance self-deception, contradictory beliefs, aphasias, loss of memory, compulsions, ignorance about one's motives and intentions, dreaming and sleepwalking, the subconscious, schizophrenia, and dissociative personality (p. 279).

While I am in broad agreement with Margolis here, in the following chapter I will suggest that dissociative personality, and in particular Multiple Personality Disorder, may not be compatible with the ascription of a single mind.

By contrast with the singularity of mind, the integration of mind is *always* a matter of degree. Thus, there is no all-or-nothing difference between split-brain patients and the rest of us in this respect—we just have a higher degree of mental integration. I will argue that split-brain patients have sufficient mental integration to count as having a single mind. This claim is vindicated when we recall the comparative effects of the various forms of commissurotomy—complete, central and frontal. The important point is that the degree of psychological compartmentalization is proportionate to the amount of surgery performed. So we do not have an all-or-nothing distinction between intact and split brains, but a spectrum of degrees of coherence and compartmentalization. However, as I have stated, a single mind can be maintained even through a complete commissurotomy. To see why, let us examine the two-mind theory's account of the lack of frequent and visible conflicts between their purportedly separate minds. Puccetti, the most radical of the two-mind theorists, points out that not only do the two disconnected hemispheres have a history of almost identical experience and access to sensory stimuli, but also:

common sub-routines of learned behavior stored in the still-intact cerebellum, and a common mileau (blood sugar, hormones, etc.)... the same autonomic, humoral and muscular reactions are shared, either by peripheral sensory feedback or via the intact brain stem, the shared vascular system, cerebrospinal fluid, and so on. Since the primary drives are mediated at subcortical levels, it is no surprise that both hemispheres feel hungry, thirsty, lustful, or what have you, at the same time. Even in test conditions an emotional reaction gets into both hemispheres ([1973], p. 343).

However, surely all this counts *against* the two-mind theory. Since the brainstem and other subcortical structures are not sectioned, then both alleged 'minds' share common physical parts, and thus the mental functions and states supervenient upon them, and so these 'minds' are not distinct and separate.

The two-mind theorists forgot that while the cerebral cortex can be described as the 'seat' of conscious experience, the brain stem is a necessary condition for such experience. To quote Pallis:

The reticular formation forms the central core of the brain stem and projects to wide areas of the limbic system and neo-cortex. Projections from the upper part of the brain stem are responsible for alerting mechanisms. These can be thought of as the capacity for generating consciousness. The content of consciousness (what a person knows, thinks, feels) is a function of activated cerebral hemispheres. But unless there is a functioning brain stem 'switching on' the hemispheres, one cannot speak of such a content (p. 7).

Penfield (in Eccles [1970]) is equally explicit:

Consciousness continues, regardless of what area of cerebral cortex is removed. On the other hand, consciousness is inevitably lost when the function of the higher brain stem (diencephalon) is interrupted by injury, pressure, disease, or local epileptic discharge (p. 234).

However, we are still left with my hypothetical experiment, which strongly suggests that split-brain patients have two minds. Since I disagree with this conclusion, I am committed to showing an error in this example, as expressed in statements 1–5. For my solution to this problem, recall my example of my simultaneously both knowing and not knowing a phone number. This is clearly a case of psychological compartmentalization that is insufficient for the ascription of two minds. However, my point derives from my remark that an impersonal description of this situation could be given in neuroscientific vocabulary (e.g., without mentioning any subjects of experience), thus avoiding any appearance of contradiction as arose within the mentalistic description. My point is that this can be done regarding the results of commissurotomy.

When these results were described in folk-psychological terms (e.g., 'the patient saw both only red and only green'), it seemed that we could only avoid paradox at the expense of rejecting the idea of a single subject of experience. This, of course, was the source of the philosophical perplexity. However, when we describe the case in neuroscientific language the contradiction disappears, as do the philosophical problems. These reemerge only if we attempt to translate this description back into folk-psychological vocabulary.

Bearing all this in mind, we see that I must reject premise 3 of my argument. In other words, we hold that a single person, with a single but significantly divided brain, and a single but significantly compartmentalized mind, can, under certain highly unusual and deliberately contrived circumstances, see only red and only green simultaneously. Such a person will make incompatible claims, and have incompatible beliefs (e.g., that he's only seeing red and that he's only seeing green). He will not realize his contradictory state because he doesn't believe that he is 'seeing only red and only green.'

In conclusion, we acknowledge that some 'disunity' (i.e., compartmentalization) of mind is inevitable, and that this holds to varying degrees. When it occurs against a background of general integration, i.e., when we can *generally* explain and predict such a person's behavior in terms of a single mind—then there is one single mind. This is the case with split-brain patients—one mind, although a significantly disunited one.

APPENDIX: MY PHYSICS EXAM

I end this chapter with some reflections on Parfit's thought-experiment 'My Physics Exam' [1984, p. 246]. I will follow Parfit in telling the story in the first person.

I am one of that small percentage whose linguistic functions are equally shared by both hemispheres. I possess a device that enables me to block all direct communication between my hemispheres merely by raising my eyebrows, and to reunite them by lowering each eyebrow separately. I am taking a physics exam, and have only fifteen minutes left. However, I still have one question to answer, and don't know which of two possible strategies is the appropriate one to adopt in answering it—and I don't have time for both. So I 'divide my mind,' assigning one strategy to each hemisphere, reuniting them in time to write up the best answer.

Parfit reckons that I would experience no sensation of division, as each stream of consciousness would seem to be continuous with the pre-division single stream. The only difference for each 'subject' would be the disappearance of half the visual field, and of sensation and control of half the body. As the left hemisphere works on one strategy, he can see the hand operated by the right hemisphere working at the other strategy, but is unaware of the mental processes behind the writing. It is just as if he is looking at someone else's paper, without the risk of being disqualified for cheating. When both sets of calculations are complete, there comes a time in which, in Parfit's words, "I am now about to unite my mind." Once this reunion takes place, Parfit expects that I will remember having worked on both strategies, and that both will be genuine memories.

The first point to make here is that the example is invalidated due to factual error. Each hemisphere would not lose half its visual field in such a situation, as eye, head, and neck movements would allow vision to be totally duplicated. The second problem concerns the quote above, that "I am now about to unite my mind." This is unfortunately expressed, implying the existence of some 'I,' some conscious subject of experience, over and above the two disconnected hemispheres. Certainly Parfit would not want to admit such a subject, and neither would I. Still, this action of reuniting the mind would seem to require a high degree of cooperation between the two disconnected hemispheres, thus raising the problem of how it is achieved. Perhaps one hemisphere could signal to the other 'I've finished,' and the other could reply 'So have I,' by a prear-ranged code. If not, the problem can be overcome by recasting the story, replacing Parfit's eyebrow device with a preset timing device, so that one could set it to divide the mind and to reunite it after a given time, thus relieving the hemispheres of having to arrange the reunion themselves.

In fact, this improves the thought-experiment's credibility by bringing it closer to what is currently possible. As Patricia Churchland reports, Wada has shown that we can anesthetize a sin-gle hemisphere by injecting sodium amytal into the ipselateral carotid artery, thus putting the hemisphere out of action for as long as the drug is operative. Let us imagine that a drug has been invented that can similarly block the activity of the corpus callo-sum, while leaving the hemispheres themselves intrinsically untouched, but dissociated. Let us also imagine that the process has been refined to the extent that one could put the corpus callosum out of action for ten minutes, give or take a few seconds. We can now reconstruct Parfit's story while avoiding the problem of the hemispheres 'reuniting themselves.'

CHAPTER EIGHT

DEGREES OF PSYCHOLOGICAL INTEGRITY

MPD: HISTORICAL BACKGROUND

Having cleared some misconceptions regarding 'unity of mind,' I now turn to another prima facie paradoxical condition, Multiple Personality Disorder (MPD), which is just as challenging to our assumption that each of us possesses a single mind. I will follow this with a discussion of hypnotic phenomena, and end with some reflections on various forms of psychological fragmentation displayed in normal life.

The clinician's handbook DSM-III describes MPD as consisting of:

1. The existence within an individual of two or more distinct personalities, each of which is dominant at a particular time.

2. The personality that is dominant at any particular time determines the individual's behavior.

3. Each individual personality is complex and integrated with its own unique behavior patterns and social relationships.

Thus, each personality is equipped with a complex integrated structure of memories, behavior patterns, opinions, values, etc. Each such structure has autonomy and independence from its 'cohabitees,' often to the extent of complete ignorance as to the others' existence except through indirect external channels.

MPD was originally regarded as an extreme dissociative disorder and, after numerous changes in status, this is how it is categorized at present. As Fahy says:

The nosological status of MPD was altered when it was listed as a diag-
nosis among the dissociative states in DSM-III (American Psychiatric
Association 1980) having been included as a symptom in the hysteria sec-
tion in DSM-II (APA 1968). MPD will be accorded special recognition in
ICD-10, where it will become a special diagnosis classified under the dis-
sociative disorders of memory, awareness and identity (World Health
Organization 1987) (p. 598).

The concept of 'dissociation' originally derives from the theory of
'association,' that memories were brought to conscious awareness
by the mechanism of 'association of ideas,' so that memories that
are not available by connection to such a network are 'dissociated'
from it.

There is a great deal of controversy regarding the extant of MPD
today. It seems to have reached a peak between 1840 and 1910. For
the next few decades there was scarcely a book or article to be
found on the subject, and the few that did appear usually relied on
historical cases. As Nemiah remarks regarding dissociative disorders, by the early 20th century:

"for reasons that are not entirely clear, there was a sudden loss of interest
in these clinical syndromes... such clinical apathy cannot be blamed on a
disappearance of patients suffering from the disorders, for there is no evi-
dence to suggest that the incidence of psychogenic amnesia and most of
its related clinical states has in any way diminished since that time"
(p. 1545).

However, he regards MPD as an exception, and having all but disappeared. On the other hand, a recent study (F.W. Putnam [1986])
reported that 4,000 cases were currently in treatment, with approxi-
mately 25,000 cases of MPD now existing in North America.

In the light of Nemiah's observations, given that dissociative
disorders were with us throughout this century, it seems most likely that their low profile was a consequence of major shifts in psychology and psychiatry, firstly under the impact of Freud, and later
as a result of the downplaying of 'mind' and 'consciousness' by
behaviorism. As Kuhn has made very clear, such a change in per-

spective is accompanied by a change in interests and priorities, so that what was once a central research project or field of inquiry suddenly becomes an unfashionable marginal issue, and is subsequently ignored.

Contrary to Putnam's figures stated above, it is still being argued that the present relative scarcity of MPD, and its virtual confinement to one socio-historical context, is a strong indication that MPD was an artifact of a particular social environment, and more particularly the self-fulfilling creation of a specific psychiatric theory. In other words, the suggestion is that MPD is an iatrogenic illness. For instance, in a supposedly definitive article, Charles Rycroft argues that the two necessary conditions for the development of MPD are:

1. Prevailing views on the nature of personality make it conceivable that two personalities can occupy the same bodily frame.

2. The potential case of multiple or split personality encounters a psychiatrist who believes in, or is already interested in, dissociation of the personality (p. 197).

This first alleged condition is confused. Certainly, no psychiatric condition could be categorized, nor recognized, except within a theoretical framework that regarded it as conceivable. However, this is a general point about the preconditions of perception and understanding, and thus cannot carry the critical weight that Rycroft intends of it. Secondly, if no cases had been presented to psychiatrists exhibiting symptoms like those of MPD, it is hard to see how or why any theories attempting to account for such phenomena would have been developed. In fact, many case histories clearly state that the symptoms were well-developed before the patient was presented to any psychiatrist.

Rycroft's second condition can be taken in two ways: firstly, as before, it can merely point to the fact that a theory is a lens through which we interpret experience. Secondly, it can be seen as pointing to the phenomenon of transference, whereby patients will unconsciously produce the symptoms that they think the doctor wants, in order to please him or elicit his praise. But again, this is recognized as a hazard for all forms of psychotherapy, and can be present with many psychiatric conditions, and thus cannot be employed to specifically dismiss MPD.

It has also been suggested that, given that the vast majority of historical cases exhibited a split between the original reserved uptight personality and a second (or more) fun-loving personality, then the dissociation between the two was explicable as a result of the repression of life-affirming impulses under the weight of convention and 'Victorian values.' These strictures would be reflected in the formality and reticence of the doctor/patient relationship, so that the second personality would only be revealed under the aegis of specially-designed contrivances such as hypnosis.

However, we can accept that these social conditions may have been responsible for the particular *form* that the typical split took, while maintaining that there is a *general* underlying tendency for the psyche to fragment under pressure, common to all social settings. Anyhow, Rycroft's arguments are totally beside the point. Even if MDP was a purely iatrogenic condition, and restricted to certain social environments, this does not remove the fact that it still existed. It merely offers an account of how it came to be—but whatever the cause, the effect is real.

Furthermore, we now have independent techniques with which to identify MPD, based on the recognition that such psychological conditions have certain physical accompaniments. For example, as Wilkes [1988] reports, it has been demonstrated that different 'personalities' display different responses to EEG tests; in galvanic skin response to emotionally loaded words and phrases, and in visually evoked responses to light flashes. As Humphrey & Dennett say:

What data there are all go to show that multiple patients—in the context of the clinic—may indeed undergo profound psychophysiological changes when they change personality state. There is preliminary evidence, for example, of changes in handedness, voice patterns, evoked-response brain activity, and cerebral blood flow. When samples of the different handwritings of a multiple are mixed with samples by different hands, police handwriting experts have been unable to identify them. There are data to suggest differences in allergy reactions and thyroid functioning. Drug studies have shown differences in responsivity to alcohol and tranquillizers. Tests of memory have indicated genuine cross-personality amnesia for newly acquired information (while, interestingly enough, newly acquired motor skills are carried over) (p. 156).

MINDS, PERSONS, AND PERSONALITIES

What are we to say about cases of MPD? That there are two (or more) persons coexisting in one body? That there is one person with two minds, or two selves? One person with a divided mind? Note that the range of possibilities is similar to those regarding split-brain patients. Clearly, any of these descriptions will look rather odd, as they diverge so strongly from common usage. But, as is often the case, such a conflict can be an indication of an inadequate theory being stretched out of shape by the pressure of unwieldy phenomena.

In fact, to demand a decision between the above formulations, to choose which one is 'the right one,' is to ask an empty question since they are merely equivalent descriptions of the same state of affairs, all struggling to deal with the fact that MPD poses an immense challenge for the commonsense view that each person possesses a single mind. The tendency to believe that there is some objective 'fact of the matter' to enable us to choose between these formulations is based on the error of reifying the mind or the self, i.e., of viewing them as *things*. Incidentally, it should be noted that in non-philosophical discussion of these issues, the terms 'mind' and 'self' are used fairly interchangeably, with the more generally cognitive aspects stressed in the case of 'mind,' and the more reflexive aspects for 'self.' I hope this informality will not cause confusion. Indeed, some degree of looseness is inevitable with such basic psychological concepts.

In line with my conclusions in Chapter 7, I will also claim that there is no clear-cut black-and-white difference between someone with MPD and the rest of us, merely different shades of grey. In other words, the integrity of the mind is a matter of degree, with each individual being located at some point on an integration-fragmentation continuum. In fact, this follows directly from Reductionist theses 1–3. At one end we have the unattainable ideal of a perfectly integrated psyche that fully exemplifies the Socratic maxim of "Man, know thyself." At the other extreme, we have a state of total fragmentation exemplified not by MPD, but by someone like the Korsakoff victim William Thompson (see Chapter 6), who cannot in any real sense be said to have a self at all.

Due to the inherent vagueness of the central folk-psychological terms involved (see Reductionist thesis 5), we cannot give a clear demarcation line (except in a purely stipulative way) that would state precisely up to what degree of fragmentation we could regard a mind as being single. However, there are clearly some cases that seem to be beyond the pale. It is to these that I shall now turn.

MARY AND MARY

Let us consider the famous case of Mary Reynolds (1793–1854), as described by McDougal. At the age of eighteen, this young woman 'of dull and melancholy temperament' awoke from a long sleep with a severe and wide-ranging amnesia regarding episodic, semantic, and procedural memory. For example, she remembered nothing of her past life, was unable to recognize her family, and could no longer read nor write. The other most noticeable factor was that she now displayed a strikingly different personality, being 'friendly, merry and adventurous, with a new interest in the outdoors.'

I will call her original personality 'MR1,' and her new one 'MR2.' When I want to refer to her without implying any split, I will simply call her Mary. Five weeks later, following another prolonged sleep, she awoke as MR1. All her old pre-MR2 memories were now restored, but she now had total amnesia regarding the previous five weeks as MR2. She alternated between these two mutually amnesic modes for another sixteen years before stabilizing as a 'modified' MR2, where she remained for the rest of her life.

The case for MR1 and MR2 being regarded as two distinct minds focuses on the self-containment and integrity of structure of each personality. In order to explain any act performed by Mary as MR1, we would attempt to rationalize it in terms of the beliefs and desires of MR1 alone. Those of MR2 would be irrelevant, being as causally separated from those of MR1 as are those of any other person.

Relating to this, another reason for regarding MR1 and MR2 as being two separate minds is that any attempt to combine their two respective networks of mental states leads to contradiction. Take some fact 'p' that is discovered (and thus is known and believed) by MR1, but not by MR2. If we deny the distinctness of MR1 and MR2, we are forced to say that Mary both knows and does not know (and both believes and does not believe) that p at time t. As we have seen from my example of my both knowing and not knowing a phone number (in Chapter 7), such a prima facie paradoxical result does not logically imply a plurality of minds. However, unlike this previous case, in which there was a lack of integration between two different modes of information acquisition and recall, Mary presents us with the appearance of two fully formed subjects, where the disparity concerns the same fact and the same mode of knowing. This phenomenon is even more clearly illustrated in cases of intraconsciousness, to be discussed shortly.

The mutual amnesia and noncooperation between the two personae provide strong evidence against them being different aspects of a single mind. Imagine that MR1 discovers some fact, p again, that she reckons MR2 could not be trusted to keep secret. So MR1 destroys or alters the material evidence for p, making it look that not-p is the case. This external rearrangement would be sufficient to prevent MR2 from acquiring the knowledge or belief that p. MR1 acted in the knowledge that the mutual amnesia between MR2 and herself would prevent MR2 from having direct access to MR1's knowledge of p. Clearly there is a paradox in the idea of a complete and conscious self-deception—roughly, if I know enough to devise such a deception and to carry it off, then I'll know too much to be fooled by it. So given that MR1's deception of MR2 succeeds completely, and was deliberately adopted by MR1, it cannot be a case of *self*-deception, and thus we are forced to regard MR1 and MR2 as distinct and separate minds.

ALL ABOUT EVE

I now turn to a second, equally famous case of MPD, involving Ms. Chris Costner Sizemore (see Thigpen & Cleckley). Her extreme dissociation was characterized as between two highly distinct personalities, the outgoing, direct 'Eve Black,' and the timid, constrained 'Eve White.' Unlike Mary Reynolds, this is not a case of two personae alternating in a state of complete mutual amnesia. Rather, their relationship exhibited one-sided 'intraconsciousness,' where one personality is aware of the other and her thoughts throughout, even when this other is dominant or 'manifested.' Eve Black (EB) was intraconscious of Eve White (EW), while EW was totally unaware of EB's existence. As EB said, "I know her thoughts like she knows them herself. I don't think 'em, of course. But I can nearly always tell what's on her mind." Therefore, EB could somehow distinguish EW's thoughts from her own. Thus EW was 'transparent' to EB, like a case of complete telepathy, yet EB was a total stranger to EW— she had no more access to EB's thoughts than to those of any other person, and had no direct evidence of her omniscient shadow. EB's domination of EW had a further striking aspect: By some peculiar form of intense concentration, EB could 'erase' certain of EW's memories, should she decide that EW not be permitted access to them; yet she, EB, would still retain these memories.

Wilkes [1988] examines the famous Beauchamp case in terms of Dennett's six 'Conditions of Personhood' to see if these encourage a singular or plural view of the patient. I will do the same for Chris Sizemore.

For Dennett, each of the following is a necessary condition of personhood:

1. Being rational
2. Possessing states of consciousness, allowing the ascription of intentional predicates

3. Being regarded by others with a certain attitude constitutive of personhood, relating to the ascription of moral agency
   4. Having the ability to reciprocate this attitude to others.
   5. Being a language user
   6. Having self-consciousness

Firstly, on Dennett's condition 1, both EW and EB are clearly capable of rational thought to the degree required of persons. On 2, states of consciousness can be ascribed to them, as can intentional ascriptions. On 5, both are capable of verbal communication. On 6, both can be ascribed self-consciousness, as can be seen from EB's ability to distinguish 'her' thoughts from those of EW. As Wilkes notes, 3 is more problematic in its application to personalities. Regarding whether we treat such personalities as objects of moral concern, then, as Wilkes admits, "It is just a plain fact that the doctors in charge treat these patients as single individuals to be cured" (p. 121). The paradox is that at this point at the commencement of treatment, where distinct personalities are dissociated, the doctor may not have a single person there to treat. The recovery (or is it the creation?) of such an integrated individual is the whole purpose of therapy. In other words, if a doctor is presented with either EW or EB, then who, or where, is Chris Sizemore? On the other hand, the treatment will also involve the doctor taking the intentional stance towards individual personalities, e.g., in his attitude to one personality regarding *her* attitudes towards another personality. This final point shows that 4, the ability to reciprocate the intentional stance and view others as persons, is satisfied by such personalities, thus encouraging a plural view of such patients.

DISSOCIATION AND HYPNOSIS

Cases of MPD with intraconsciousness have distinct parallels with conditions that can be induced by hypnosis. Such parallels focus on the much-documented but little understood phenomenon of post-hypnotic suggestion, where commands given while the patient is in a hypnotic state will be acted upon when he is brought out of that state by means of some pre-planted cue. The person will not remember having received these instructions, and will thus be unaware of the true cause of his relevant actions. If the action is innocuous or unremarkable (e.g., lighting a cigarette after the hypnotist scratches his head), then he will rationalize his action, for example by saying that he just felt a sudden desire to smoke. He will not be lying—this is what it will feel like from the inside. However, if the action is bizarre—like one incident I witnessed in which an unfortunate victim of a stage hypnotist suddenly jumped bolt upright in the middle of the audience, screaming "The Russians are coming!"—such an action, totally incongruous in terms of his character, and his ordinary beliefs and desires, would soon be seen for what it was.

We can see similarities to EW/EB, both in terms of a split in consciousness with one-way amnesia, and with inaccessible information surfacing to directly affect behavior. But the strongest parallel is with intraconsciousness. If we take some person 'A,' and call him 'AH' when hypnotized, and 'AW' when he is out of the hypnotic trance but still vulnerable to post-hypnotic suggestion, we can say that AW performs an action whose roots are completely unknown to him. Since observing the cue is a necessary condition of the action (and since such cues can be subtle and undemonstrative, implying that someone must be watching out for it on some level), and given that AW is unaware of the cue's significance, all this suggests that some residue of AH remains while AW is dominant. This suggests that A's condition is not that of having two alternating personalities, but more closely resembles a one-way intraconscious pair like EW and EB. Of course, any split in A is much more limited, and AH is not complex enough to be regarded as a personality, as his sphere of operation is restricted to acting on a single cue. So AH is better described as an intraconscious dissociated response mechanism.

While acknowledging the similarities between hypnotic states and MPD, the actual relationship (if any) between them is unclear. As Fahy says:

Since hypnosis has been used to treat MPD it has been important to clarify the extent to which it is responsible for the disorder. Under hypnosis, alternate personalities may reveal themselves when required by the therapist. That there is a relationship between hypnosis and MPD is suggested by the high hypnotizibility scores of most MPD patients (p. 601).

Subjects under hypnosis have various features in common with MPD patients, e.g., production of alternates with different behavior patterns and amnesia, the appearance of such phenomena as automatic writing and post-hypnotic suggestion, and also:

7% of normal individuals were able to respond to suggestions to create a second personality using an age regression test.... However, the age regression model, like the automatic writing model, does not provide an entirely satisfactory comparison with MPD, lacking the complexity and chronicity of the clinical syndrome. There is scanty evidence that short-term exposure to hypnosis can induce well-developed alternates through the use of hypnosis alone.... That patients are excellent hypnotic subjects and prone to self-hypnosis does not prove that the relationship between hypnosis and MPD is causal (p. 601).

Hypnosis offers clear examples of the seemingly paradoxical states of simultaneously 'knowing and not knowing,' 'seeing and not seeing,' that resemble split-brain phenomena. For example, as Wilkes tells us, one way of finding out whether someone is really hypnotized or is faking it is to place an object like a chair in his path. The faker will walk into it, whereas the genuinely hypnotized person will walk round it. The peculiarity of this response lies in the fact that the person clearly sees the chair (as is shown by his ability to avoid colliding with it), yet he also acts as if he never saw it, as is suggested by the fact that he will not mention the chair if asked to list the contents of the room. It is also suggested by the fact that if he is asked why he diverted from his straight path, he will rationalize his action without reference to the chair.

Another striking parallel with split-brains is hypnotic anaesthesia. Hilgard [1977a] describes tests wherein a person is hypnotized and told that he will feel no pain. His arm is placed in a container of iced water, whereupon he continues to appear without distress. Even if asked, he will reply that he feels nothing. However, if he is asked to write his answer to this question using his other hand, which is placed out of his sight, he will complain bitterly about the pain. This 'writer' is commonly referred to as the 'hidden observer.' So here is a case of someone who simultaneously both feels and does not feel pain. This case has a variety of philosophical implications. Not least, it is commonly assumed that first-person pain reports are incorrigible. In other words, it is assumed that you cannot possibly be mistaken regarding whether or not you are now in pain. (Of course, you can be mistaken about what type of pain it is, or about the cause of the pain, e.g., phantom limbs.)

THE SELF

Discussion of 'the self' in contemporary clinical psychotherapy does not presuppose the existence of some entity of that name, over and above facts about physical and psychological continuity. As Toulmin says, we must distinguish this project from that of the speculative philosophical psychology of the past, which postulated the self as a theoretical entity in order to explain the order and regularity among mental contents—an enterprise doomed to failure, as Hume recognized. To quote Toulmin:

In clinical contexts, the point of invoking the self is not to speculate about concealed mechanisms.... Theories of the self 'cash in for' a special class of empirical relations within the whole spectrum of 'self'-phenomena: self-esteem, self-control, self-understanding, etc. (p. 308).

So talk of 'self' has no hypothetical nor explanatory overtones, but is descriptive and diagnostic, and provides both a grounding and an extension of everyday talk on reflexive attitudes. In other words, the concept of 'self' is an abstraction from these relations.

Rather than dwelling on the question of the existence of the self, a clinical theory of self is primarily concerned with the integration or fragmentation of one's cognitive structure. Toulmin again:

To be mature (or free from psychological troubles) is to have a 'cohesive, well-integrated self'; to suffer from psychological immaturities (or difficulties in the area of self-knowledge) is to have a 'fragile, fragmented, and/or incompletely cohesive self' (p. 309).

This is reflected in such common expressions as 'cracking up,' 'falling apart' or, conversely, 'being together'.

Toulmin's position fits well with my Reductionist theory of mind and self, since:

The integration of the cohesive self is the compendious label for the coherence of feelings and motives, intentions and actions, typical of a psychologically free agent... [consisting in]... a rational coherence between the different components of his self-knowledge... Conversely, fragmentation of the self [consists in]... the absence of intelligible coherence between these different reflexive characteristics of the agent's conduct (p. 309).

A MATTER OF DEGREE

Perhaps one day, when a fully satisfactory neuroscience is developed, MPD will be given an explanation that dissolves its apparently paradoxical nature, where, instead of positing two or more 'minds' or 'selves,' we could describe the dissociated physical processes impersonally. However, for the moment we must accept that 'the information currently available concerning neurophysiological processes is not sufficiently detailed to provide clinically useful concepts and explanations" (Nemiah, p. 1545). We can now see why MPD remains a source of philosophical perplexity. Like split-brain phenomena (and also alexia, visual agnosia, etc.) it is inexplicable in terms of folk-psychological vocabulary, with its assumption of a single conscious agent—but unlike these conditions, the commonsense model has not been superseded by a more scientific explanation. Any explanations regarding MPD tend to be based on possible causative factors in the social sphere.

I will now develop my position, parallel to that of Chapter 7, that those with MPD are not distinguished from the rest of us by having a different number of entities that can be called 'minds' or 'selves,' but that we occupy different positions on a continuum of psychological integration-fragmentation. I will do so by examining a range of mental phenomena experienced by people in general, i.e., not only clinical cases. As an entry to this survey, I will mention a causative account of MPD as suggested by Glover. He notes that contemporary documented cases indicate that MPD is often linked with a history of child abuse. He argues plausibly that:

It may be very hard to form a single picture of yourself that includes both normal relationships... and your role as the victim of these assaults. One way of coping with this would be to compartmentalize your life, behaving as different people in different contexts (p. 23).

By comparison, Glover draws our attention to well documented cases of those who worked in Nazi concentration camps, as doctors, etc.. They participated in, or turned a blind eye to, the most hideously evil deeds, yet returned home at night to resume life as a loving husband and father. One would not want to say that such a person had two minds or selves, since, unlike MPD, there is no mutual amnesia between the two sets of stages. However, even against this background of integration, there is clearly a substantial degree of dissociation involved, and this should not surprise us— how else would one cope with the contradictions of such a life? And let us not be complacent or superior. No one familiar with the work of Stanley Milgram (where the majority of subjects proved themselves willing to torture someone to death in obedience to authority) can assume that they would be any different. These camp workers were not essentially evil or 'different' from ourselves—they were ordinary people like you and I responding to extraordinary conditions.

Glover quotes Robert Jay Lifton, who describes the camp worker's situation as involving 'doubling,' i.e., where a psychological barrier is set up so that the two highly conflicting modes of being, the sadistic torturer and the family man, are felt as being nothing to do with each other. Thus they are turned into two mutually exclusive modes of being, and never co-experienced. Such a person leaves his humanity at the gates as he 'clocks in' to the mode of camp worker, and collects it again as he sheds his worker mode at the end of his shift. Lifton uses the term 'doubling' to draw attention to the fact that it involves "the creation of two autonomous selves." In other words, there is a high degree of integration within each 'self,' but little communication between each 'self.' This dissociation does not hold to such a high degree as in MPD, but there are strong enough similarities between them to warrant the suggestion that MPD is a more extreme development of a general tendency of the psyche to fragment under pressure.

Moving along the continuum towards the ideal state of integration, we come to ourselves. We all know the guy who is a subservient doormat at the office and a tyrant at home. Is this not just a less extreme example of what Lifton is talking about? It is always much easier to see such compartmentalization in others! But it is now a commonplace that people adopt different roles and behavior patterns in different types of situations, with little self-awareness or appreciation of doing so. We all express fragmentation of this kind to some degree. One of the most penetrating observations of this everyday condition comes not from the world of professional philosophy, psychology, or psychotherapy, but from the enigmatic Armenian sage G.I. Gurdjieff. I include his description of the average person's state of psychological integration because it makes an interesting comparison with Lifton, not least in the similarity between their metaphors of 'barriers' and 'buffers':

'Buffer' is a term which requires special explanation. We know what buffers on railway carriages are. They are contrivances which lessen the shock when carriages or trucks touch one another. If there were no buffers the shock of one carriage against another would be very unpleasant and dangerous. Buffers soften the results of these shocks and render them unnoticeable and imperceptible. Exactly the same appliances are to be found in man.... The cause of their appearance is the existence in man of many contradictions...of opinions, feelings, sympathies, words and actions. If a man throughout the whole of his life were to feel all the con-

tradictions that are within him he could not live and act as calmly as he
lives and acts now. He would have constant friction, constant unrest... but
if buffers are created in him he can cease to feel them, and he will not feel
the impact from the clash of contradictory views, contradictory emotions,
contradictory words (Ouspensky, P. 154).

These groups of thoughts and feelings separated by buffers are not substantial enough to count as 'selves' or 'minds.' They are best described as roles or sub-personae, and represent the far less drastic degree of fragmentation found in normal life, without the greater pressures of the concentration camp worker. Such 'buffers' are not static structures, but are dynamic, adapting to new experiences. Nor are they indestructible, although their dismantling is a tricky business. However, a successful dismantling of buffers will allow one to achieve a greater integrity of thought, feeling and action, free from the internal coercive agencies that characterize such a departmentalization of experience, and will lead us up the continuum towards what Toulmin calls 'maturity.' This is, of course, the aim of all forms of psychotherapy, and an aim of any genuine spiritual discipline. Of course, 'buffers' do not exist any more than do 'selves,' over and above the existence of beliefs, desires, etc. The utility of the concept is to mark a form of fragmentation between these.

To end this chapter, I will clear up a few loose ends regarding self-deception, as this offers another angle into the relative fragmentation of the psyche in everyday life. As we have seen, there is a paradox in the idea that one mind can consciously and completely achieve self-deception, and it was the existence of a consciously applied strategy, successfully applied, that made it impossible to characterize the hypothetical deception of MR1 over MR2 as *self*-deception, and therefore why we had to regard MR1 and MR2 as distinct minds. However, it remains true that, despite any paradox, we all believe that self-deception is an uncomfortably common occurrence. I agree with Glover that the seeming plausibility of a complete conscious self-deception derives from an unconscious amalgamation of two different, lesser forms of self-deception.

Firstly we have a self-deception that is conscious but incomplete, i.e., where one suspects that something is the case, but deliberately avoids investigating the matter thoroughly, nor spells out to oneself the consequences of its being so. Consider a form of self-deception I imposed on myself recently: I noticed that I had developed a small but painful lump on my body. After an immediate panic of "Oh, no, I've got cancer!" I found myself deliberately ignoring it, not examining it, not going to the doctor, and immediately blocking any awareness of it. This situation continued for several weeks until the strain of the pretence forced me to find out what the lump was, to my relief.

Secondly we have a self-deception that is complete, but unconsciously performed, i.e., where we unconsciously ignore evidence that, with hindsight, was staring us in the face, but would have been denied had someone suggested it at the time. For example, after a relationship has ended, you can often recognize certain events as signifying the beginning of the end, or as having an import that was not admitted at the time, through unconsciously choosing to ignore an unpleasant truth.

IN CONCLUSION

The pivotal point in the book has been Chapter 5, where I have urged a reconfiguration of the entire study of personal identity. I am sure that anyone who has worked with the traditional problems of self and identity by employing the typical thought-experimental problem cases has been subject to worries about the value of their answers. How could such artificial and contrived examples tell us anything relevant or important about ourselves? I have tried to expose the roots of these worries. I have attempted to show that any such conclusions are firstly unreliable, given their dependence on our intuitions; and secondly inconclusive, as an equally ingenious counterexample seems always to be available. This way of doing things, which has characterized the study from the beginning, has run its course. Anything that can be learned from this methodology has been assimilated long ago. We need to reorient the entire debate.

Let me be quite explicit here. I am saying that the traditional problems of personal identity are largely pseudo-problems that are the result of an inappropriate methodology. To get to the genuine and interesting problems of personal identity, this methodology must be dropped, or at least placed under tight limitations.

I have suggested that we dismantle the 'problem of personal identity' itself, by showing how traditionally problematic issues stem from an unwise emphasis on counterfactual 'puzzle cases.' These cases were created by devising situations in which our usual bodily and mental continuities were separated or placed in conflict with each other, thereby creating opposing 'criteria of personal identity,' only one of which could be correct. This error was associated with the employment of far too loose a conception of possibility, regarding whether or not these hypothetical states of affairs could actually occur. This in turn led to a false estimation of the relevance of these examples to the issues.

Once these 'criteria' cease to be placed in artificial opposition, then we can accept the Physical Criterion as embodying the commonsense view that we are essentially material beings, and that the survival of one and the same person is typically marked by the physical continuity of a single body. Within this, we can acknowledge the unique significance of the brain. I remain agnostic over the possibility of brain transplants. Should they occur, then I accept the judgment that I go where my brain goes. Pushing my liberalism regarding thought-experiments to the limit, I would say that should 'brain division' and cerebral hemisphere transplants ever take place, so that two surviving persons have portions of my brain, then Parfit's analysis is largely correct.

Regarding the Psychological Criterion, the issues that remain center on the concepts of psychological integration and psychological continuity, concerning respectively the copersonality of mental events at-a-time, and over time. The important point is that these issues will be located *within the sciences*. For example, the philosophical problems deriving from amnesia or split-brain research are both located within the neuro-sciences. The problems deriving from MPD take place within psychiatry. In order to make a useful contribution to these studies, philosophers will have to become more familiar with the relevant areas of scientific research than we have (with notable exceptions) shown ourselves to have been in the past. Thankfully, there is growing recognition of this fact.

The philosophical contribution will primarily involve an investigation into the relationships between
i. our commonsense concepts and theories
ii. our inherited philosophical theories
iii. the results of scientific research, and their interpretation within scientific concepts and theories

In this enterprise, the role of the philosopher is to provide and encourage advice, conciliation, and arbitration: determining errors, agreements, misunderstandings and, where there are irreconcilable differences, to delimit the domain of each party. This will be done with the crucial acknowledgement that the philosopher is not thereby making judgements from 'on high,' i.e., from some perspective above or prior to that of the empirical sciences. It is rather from the ground floor level, working with scientists from within the given field of enquiry, with each engaged in different but complementary aspects of the same enterprise.

SUGGESTED FURTHER READING

Chapter 1 An excellent anthology covering all the issues discussed in this book is Kolak and Martin [1991]. Historical sources are gathered in Perry [1975]. The single most important work on personal identity in recent years is Parfit [1984], especially Part 3.

Chapter 2 Williams [1970] and Lewis [1976] are in Kolak and Martin, as are relevant sections of Parfit, Nozick [1981], and Unger [1990].

Chapter 3 Locke and Butler can be found in Perry. Swinburne is best represented in Shoemaker & Swinburne [1984]. Flew [1987] is a good collection on the implications of parapsychology.

Chapter 4 Wiggins [1980]; Brennan [1988]; Parfit, op.cit.

Chapter 5 Wilkes [1988]; Unger [1990]—especially the first chapter of both.

Chapter 6 Locke, Parfit, op.cit. Tragic but fascinating brain disorders are described in Sacks [1986].

Chapter 7. For general background on the brain, see Churchland [1986]. A good (and very short) book on commissurotomy is Marks [1986]; also Nagel [1971] and Sperry [1968b] in Kolak and Martin.

Chapter 8 On MPD, see Humphrey and Dennett [1989], and Chapter 4 of Wilkes [1988], both reprinted in Kolak and Martin. For hypnosis, see the section of Hilgard [1977] in Kolak and Martin. For self-deception, see Haight [1980], and Martin [1985].

BIBLIOGRAPHY

Baillie, James [1990a] 'Identity, Survival, and Sortal Concepts,' *Philosophical Quarterly, Vol 40*

Baillie, James [1990b] 'The Problem of Personal Identity,' *Cogito, Vol 4, No 2*

Baillie, James [1990c] 'Philosophical Problems of the Self,' *The Psychologist, Vol 3, No 7*

Baillie, James [1991] 'Split Brains and Single Minds,' *Journal of Philosophical Research, Vol XVI*

Brennan, Andrew [1988] *Conditions of Identity*, Oxford: Clarendon Press

Butler, Joseph [1736] 'Of Personal Identity,' in Perry

Campbell, Jeremy [1982] *Grammatical Man*, Simon & Schuster

Churchland, Patricia [1986] *Neurophilosophy*, MIT Press

Churchland, Paul [1988] 'How Parapsychology Could Become a Science,' *Inquiry, Vol 30*

Dennett, Daniel [1976] 'Conditions of Personhood,' in his *Brainstorms*, Bradford Books 1978

DeWitt, Larry [1975] 'Consciousness, Mind, and Self,' *British Journal of the Philosophy of Science, Vol 26*

Diagnostic and Statistical Manual III [1980], American Psychiatric Association

Eccles, John [1970] 'Brain and Conscious Experience,' in his *Facing Reality; Philosophical Adventures by a Brain Scientist*, Springer Verlag

Eccles, John & Popper, Karl [1977] *The Self and its Brain*, Springer Verlag

Evans, Gareth [1982] *The Varieties of Reference*, Oxford, Clarendon Press

Fahy, T.A. [1988] 'The Diagnosis of MPD: A Critical Review,' *British Journal of Psychiatry, Vol 153*

Flew, Antony [1951] 'Locke and the Problem of Personal Identity,' *Philosophy, 1951*

Flew, Antony [1987] *Readings in the Philosophical Problems of Parapsychology*, Prometheus Books

Foster, John [1979] 'In Self-Defence,' in *Perception and Identity*, Ed. G.F. McDonald, Oxford: Clarendon Press

Gazzaniga, M. [1970] *The Bisected Brain*, Plenum Press, New York

Gazzaniga, M. & LeDoux, J. [1978] *The Integrated Mind*, Plenum Press, New York

Gillett, Grant [1986] 'Brain Bisection and Personal Identity,' *Mind, Vol. 95*

Glover, Jonathan [1988] *"I": The Philosophy and Psychology of Personal Identity*, Penguin

Gregory, R.L. [1987] (Ed.) *Oxford Companion to the Mind*, Oxford University Press, Oxford

Haight, M.R. [1980] *A Study in Self-Deception*, Atlantic Highlands, N.J.: Humanities Press

Hilgard, E. [1977a] *Divided Consciousness*, John Wiley & Sons, London

Hilgard [1977b] 'Dissociative Phenomena and the Hidden Observer,' in Hilgard [1977a] and in Kolak & Martin

Hume, David [1739] *A Treatise on Human Nature* (Ed. L.A. Selby-Bigge, 1965), Oxford: Clarendon Press

Humphrey, Nicholas, & Dennett, Daniel [1989] 'Speaking for Ourselves: An Assessment of Multiple Personality Disorder,' *Raritan: A Quarterly Review, IX,* and in Kolak & Martin

James, William [1890] *Principles of Psychology*, Dover Press, N.Y.

Kolak, Daniel, & Martin, Raymond [1990] *Self & Identity*, Macmillan

Kuhn, Thomas [1962] *The Structure of Scientific Revolutions*, University of Chicago Press

Levy, J.; Trevarthan, C.; Sperry, R. [1972] 'Perception of Bilateral Chimeric Figures Following Hemispheric Disconnection,' *Brain, Vol 95*

Lewis, D.K. [1976] 'Survival and Identity' in his *Philosphical Papers, Vol 1*, Oxford: Clarendon Press; also in Kolak & Martin

Lifton, Robert Jay [1987] *The Future of Immorality*, New York

Locke, John [1694] *An Essay Concerning Human Understanding, 2nd Ed.*

(Ed. P.H. Nidditch), Oxford, Clarendon Press

Madell, Geoffrey [1981] *The Identity of the Self,* Edinburgh University Press

Margolis, Joseph [1975] 'Puccetti on Minds, Brains and Persons,' *British Journal of the Philosophy of Science, 26*

Marks, Charles [1986] *Commissurotomy, Consciousness & Unity of Mind,* MIT Press

McDougal, W. [1926] *Outline of Abnormal Psychology,* Methuen

Milgram, Stanley [1974] *Obedience to Authority,* Harper and Row

Nagel, Thomas [1971] 'Brain Bisection and the Unity of Consciousness,' in his *Mortal Questions,* Cambridge University Press, 1979; also in Kolak & Martin

Nagel, Thomas [1986] *The View from Nowhere,* Oxford, Clarendon Press

Nemiah, J. [1980] 'Dissociative Disorders,' in *Comprehensive Textbook of Psychiatry, 3rd Ed.,* Kaplan, Freedman & Siddick, Williams Press

Nozick, Robert [1981] *Philosophical Explanations,* Oxford, Clarendon Press

Ouspensky, P.D. [1950] *In Search of the Miraculous,* Routledge and Kegan Paul

Pallis, C. [1983] 'ABC of Brain Stem Death,' *British Journal of Medicine*

Parfit, Derek [1971] 'Personal Identity,' in Perry

Parfit, Derek [1976], 'Lewis, Perry, and What Matters,' in Rorty

Parfit, Derek [1984] *Reasons and Persons,* Oxford: Clarendon Press

Penfield, W. & Rasmussen, T. [1957] *The Cerebral Cortex of Man,* Macmillan

Perry, John [1975] (Ed.) *Personal Identity,* University of California Press

Psychiatric Clinics of America [1984] *Symposium on Multiple Personality*

Puccetti, Roland [1973] 'Brain Bisection and Personal Identity,' *British Journal of the Philosophy of Science, 24*

Puccetti, Roland [1975] 'The Mute Self,' *British Journal of the Philosophy of Science, 26*

Putnam, F.W. [1986] 'The Clinical Phenomenology of Multiple Personality Disorder: Review of 100 recent cases,' *Journal of Clinical Psychiatry, Vol 47*

Putnam, Hilary [1970] 'Is Semantics Possible?,' in his *Mind, Language, and Reality,* Cambridge University Press 1975

Reid, Thomas [1785] 'On Mr. Locke's Account of Personal Identity,' in Perry

Robinson, John [1988] 'Personal Identity and Survival,' *Journal of*

Philosophy

Rorty, Amelie [1976] *The Identities of Persons,* University of California Press

Rycroft, Charles [1987] 'Dissocation of Personality,' in Gregory

Sacks, Oliver [1986] *The Man Who Mistook His Wife for a Hat,* Harper and Row

Shoemaker, S. & Swinburne, R. [1984] *Personal Identity,* Basil Blackwell

Sperry, Roger [1968a] 'Mental Unity following Surgical Disconnection of the Cerebral Hemispheres,' *Harvey Lectures, 62*

Sperry, Roger [1968b] 'Hemisphere Deconnection and Unity in Conscious Awareness,' *American Psychologist, 23,* and in Kolak & Martin

Swinburne, Richard [1974] 'Personal Identity,' *Proceedings of the Aristotelian Society, 1974*

Thigpen, C.H. & Cleckley, H. [1957] *The Three Faces of Eve,* Popular Library, New York

Toulmin, Stephen [1977] 'Self-Knowledge of the Self,' in *The Self,* Ed. Theodore Mischel, Basil Blackwell, Oxford

Unger, Peter [1990] *Identity, Consciousness and Value,'* Oxford University Press

Wheatley, J.M.O. & Edge, H.L. [1976] *Philosophical Dimensions of Para-Psychology,* Charles Thomas, New York

Wiggins, David [1980] *Sameness and Substance,* Basil Blackwell, Oxford

Wilkes, Kathleen [1978] 'Consciousness and Commissurotomy,' *Philosophy 53*

Wilkes, Kathleen [1988] *Real People,* Oxford: Clarendon Press

Williams, Bernard [1957] 'Personal Identity and Individuation,' in Williams [1973]

Williams, Bernard [1970] 'The Self and the Future,' in Williams [1973], and in Kolak & Martin

Williams, Bernard [1973] *Problems of the Self,* Cambridge University Press

Zaidel, E [1975] 'A Technique for presenting Lateralized Vision Input with Prolonged Exposure,' *Vision Research 15*

INDEX OF NAMES

Aristotle: 58

Arnauld, A: 51

Ayer, A.J: 42

Bogen, J: 126–7

Brennan, A: 20, 24, 30, 71–6, 106

Butler, J: 40–2

Churchland, Patricia: 121, 140

Churchland, Paul: 56

Dennett, D: 144, 148–9

Descartes, R: 51, 59, 62, 82, 101

DeWitt, L: 128–9

Eccles, J: 125–8

Evans, G: 43

Fahy, T: 140; 150–1

Flew, A: 98–9, 111

Foster, J: 53

Freud, S: 142

Gazzaniga, M: 127–8, 130, 132

Gillett, G: 122, 132

Glover, J: 154–6

Gurdjieff, G I: 155

Hilgard, E: 151

Hume, D: 41, 42, 109, 152

Humphrey, N: 144

James, W: 112–3

Kant, I: 9

Kuhn, T: 56, 142

Ledoux, J: 132

Levy, J: 120

Lewis, D: 33–9

Lifton, R. J: 154–5

Locke, J. 30–1, 40–2, 59–63, 76–7, 79, 98–101, 103, 107, 111–2

Madell, G: 47

Margolis, J: 136

Milgram, S: 154

Nagel, T: 8, 24, 115, 125, 133

Namiah, J: 142, 153

Nozick, R: 12, 15–20, 27, 85

Pallis, C: 137

Parfit, D: 3, 8, 10, 12, 17, 20–33, 36, 43–6, 48–9, 54–6, 66–8, 71–6, 79–80, 85, 90–7, 103–6, 110, 138–9, 159

Penfield, W: 101–3, 137
Plato: 100
Price, H.H: 56
Puccetti, R: 123–5, 128–9, 136
Putnam, F.W: 142–3
Putnam, H: 63, 66, 83–4
Reid,T: 10, 30–1, 103–4
Robinson, J: 25, 27–8
Rycroft, C: 143–4
Sacks, O: 108–10
Sartre, J-P: 87
Shoemaker, S: 49, 51, 53
Sperry, R: 117, 120, 127, 129–31, 133

Swinburne, R: 46–54, 83
Toulmin, S: 152–3, 156
Trevartham, C: 120
Unger, P: 23, 84–5, 92–7
Wada, J: 140
Wiggins, D: 8, 32, 58–9, 63–7, 71, 76–7
Wilkes, K: 80–8, 120, 144, 148–9, 151
Williams, B: 12–15, 17, 20, 22, 30–3, 48, 79, 90–1
Wittgenstein, L: 3
Zaidel, E: 127–9

INDEX OF SUBJECTS

A

Amnesia: 103–13
    in MPD, 145–8
Animal Attribute View: 64

B

Brain: Chapter 7 passim
    asymptomatic agenesis of the
        corpus callosum, 134
    brain transplants, 24–6, 44–5,
        89–90, 159
    cognition in the right hemi
        sphere, 125–9
    hemisphere transplants,
        25–33
    hemispherectomy, 124
Buffers: 155–6

C

Closest Continuer Theory: 15–20
Commissurotomy: Chapter 7
    passim
    effects, 117

experiments, 119–20, 127–9,
    134–5
operation described, 115–8
Complex View: See
    Reductionism
Copying Process: , 25, 73–6
Cross-cuing: 130–1

D

Disembodied existence: 50–2, 70
Dissociation: Chapter 8 passim
Doubling: 154–5

E

Empiricist theories: See
    Reductionism
ESP: 55–6

F

Fission: Chapter 2 passim, 85–6

H

Human Beings: See Man/Person
   distinction

I

I-relation: 34–9
Identity:
   diachronic, 5
   logic of identity relation, 4–5,
      8, 33–9
   numerical, 5
   qualitative, 5
   relativity of, 76–7
   sortal dependency of, 58–9,
      67, 76–7
   synchronic: 5
   tensed: 36–9
Integration of mind: 136–8,
   153–6

K

Korsakoff syndrome: 107–10

L

Laws, natural: 63–6 Chapter 5
   passim
Law cluster concepts: 83–4
Leibniz' Law: 5–6

M

Man/Person distinction: 59–63,
   76–7
Memory: 42–6 Chapter 6 passim
MPD: Chapter 8 passim
   classifications of: 141–2
   intraconsciousness in: 147–9

N

Non-Reductionism: 7; Chapter 3
   passim

O

Only x and y rule: 30–1

P

Persons:
   conditions of personhood:
      148–9
   See also Man/Person distinc-
      tion
Phased sortal concepts: 59
Possibility:
   deep, 68
   factual, 98–9
   logical, 98–9
   technical, 68
   theoretical, 83–91, 159
Production processes: 73
Parapsychology: 54–7
Physical Criterion: defined 9–10;
   Chapter 2 passim,

Physical spectrum: 23–5
Pseudomorphism: 74
Psychogenic fugue: 112–3
Psychological Criterion: defined
    10–11; Chapters 2 and 6 passim
    alleged circularity of, 40–3
Psychological spectrum: 20–3

Q

Quasi-memory: 93–6

R

Reductionism: defined 7–8;
    Chapters 1-8 passim
Reincarnation: 54
Relation R:

S

Self-deception: 147, 156–7
Simple View: See Non-
    Reductionism
Singularity of mind: 114, 135–8
Sorites paradox: 20–1
Split-brain: See Commissurotomy
Soul: Chapter 3 passim; 59–62
Survival: Chapters 2 and 4 passim
    conditions of, 25, 71–6
    relation, 71–6
    what matters in, 91–7

T

Theseus' ship: 15–6
Teletransportation: 31, 67–71,
    73–6, 91–7
Thought-experiments: 3–4,
    Chapter 5 passim; 158–9